Word Essentials

M.L. HUMPHREY

SELECT TITLES BY M.L. HUMPHREY

CONTENTS

Word for Beginners

WORD ESSENTIALS BOOK 1

M.L. HUMPHREY

CONTENTS

INTRODUCTION

The purpose of this guide is to introduce you to the basics of using Microsoft Word. While there are a number of other word processing programs out there, Word is still the gold-standard go-to program in use in large portions of the corporate world, so if you're going to be involved in a white collar job (and even some blue collar jobs), being familiar with Word will be a significant advantage for you. And essential for many jobs. (The days of having an assistant who could do those things for you are gone.)

It's also the program I use for all of my writing. (This book isn't going to be focused on self-publishing, but if you format a document the right way in Word you can publish directly to most of the major sales platforms without any additional effort.)

Word can be incredibly simple to use. At its most basic, you can open a new file, type in your text, save, and be done. But chances are that you'll want more control over what you type and how it looks than that. Maybe you need to use a different font or font size. Maybe you want to indent your paragraphs. Maybe you want to include a bulleted or numbered list in your document.

That's where this guide comes in. I'll walk you through the absolute basics (open, save, delete), too, but most of this guide will be focused on what to do with your text once it's been typed into your document.

Having said that, we're not going to cover everything you can do in Word. The goal of this guide is to get you up to speed and comfortable with what you'll need for probably 98% of what you'll use Word for on a daily basis.

The exceptions to that are if you're working in an environment where you need to use track changes to work on a group document or one where you need to create tables or complex multilevel lists. Those are more advanced topics that are covered in *Intermediate Word*.

The goal here is to give you a solid foundation that you can work from, and I don't want to distract from those core skills by getting into specialized topics that either won't apply to most users or that require enough detail to understand that they'll likely confuse a beginning user.

Another thing to note before we get started. All of the screenshots I'm going to show you are from Word 2013. If you have an earlier version of Word, especially a version prior to 2007, things may look different at the top of the screen. All of the shortcut keys, which I would recommend you use, will be the same, but navigation won't be.

With Excel I recommend that people with older versions upgrade to a post-2007 version of the program. With Word, especially for the beginner level, that probably isn't necessary. However, if you're using a really old version of Word you're going to have less help options. Right now the Microsoft website only has tutorials for Word 2010, 2013, and 2016, and most users won't have access to your version of Word to be able to see what you're seeing.

If you're using Word 2016, nothing we're going to cover here appears to have changed with the most recent version, so you should be fine.

Alright then. Ready? Let's do this.

BASIC TERMINOLOGY

Before we get started, I want to make sure that we're on the same page in terms of terminology.

TAB

I refer to the menu choices at the top of the screen (File, Home, Insert, Design, Page Layout, References, Mailings, Review, View, Developer) as tabs. If you click on one you'll see that the way it's highlighted sort of looks like an old-time filing system.

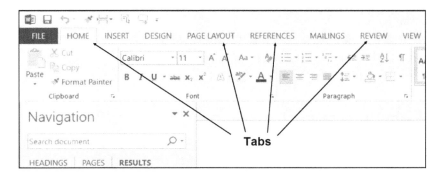

Each tab you select will show you different options. For example, in the image above, I have the Home tab selected and you can do various tasks such as cut/copy/paste, format paint, change the font, change the formatting of a paragraph, apply a style to your text, find/replace words in your document, or select the text in your document. Other tabs give other options.

CLICK

If I tell you to click on something, that means to use your mouse (or trackpad) to move the arrow on the screen over to a specific location and left-click or right-click on the option. (See the next definition for the difference between left-click and right-click).

If you left-click, this selects the item. If you right-click, this generally creates a dropdown list of options to choose from. If I don't tell you which to do, left- or right-click, then left-click.

LEFT-CLICK/RIGHT-CLICK

If you look at your mouse or your trackpad, you generally have two flat buttons to press. One is on the left side, one is on the right. If I say left-click that means to press down on the button on the left. If I say right-click that means press down on the button on the right.

Now, as I sadly learned when I had to upgrade computers and ended up with an HP Envy, not all track pads have the left- and right-hand buttons. In that case, you'll basically want to press on either the bottom left-hand side of the track pad or the bottom right-hand side of the trackpad. Since you're working blind it may take a little trial and error to get the option you want working. (Or is that just me?)

SELECT OR HIGHLIGHT

If I tell you to select text, that means to left-click at the end of the text you want to select, hold that left-click, and move your cursor to the other end of the text you want to select.

Another option is to use the Shift key. Go to one end of the text you want to select. Hold down the shift key and use the arrow keys to move to the other end of the text you want to select. If you arrow up or down, that will select an entire row at a time.

With both methods, which side of the text you start on doesn't matter. You can start at the end and go to the beginning or start at the beginning and go to the end. Just start at one end or the other of the text you want to select.

The text you've selected will then be highlighted in gray. Like the words "sample text" in this image:

This is sample text so you can see what I'm talking about.

If you need to select text that isn't touching you can do this by selecting your first section of text and then holding down the Ctrl key and selecting your second section of text using your mouse. (You can't arrow to the second section of text or you'll lose your already selected text.)

DROPDOWN MENU

If you right-click in a Word document, you will see what I'm going to refer to as a dropdown menu. (Sometimes it will actually drop upward if you're towards the bottom of the document.)

A dropdown menu provides you a list of choices to select from.

There are also dropdown menus available for some of the options listed under the tabs at the top of the screen. For example, if you go to the Home tab, you'll see small arrows below or next to some of the options, like the numbered list option in the paragraph section. If you click on those arrows, you'll see that there are multiple choices you can choose from listed on a dropdown menu.

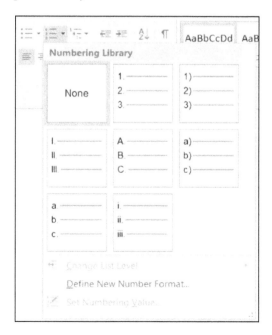

EXPANSION ARROWS

I don't know the official word for these, but you'll also notice at the bottom right corner of most of the sections in each tab that there are little arrows. If you hold your mouse over the arrow it lets you bring up a more detailed set of options, usually through a dialogue box (which we'll discuss next).

In the Home tab, for example, there are expansion arrows for Clipboard, Font, Paragraph, and Styles. Holding your mouse over the arrow will give a brief description of what clicking on the expansion arrow will do.

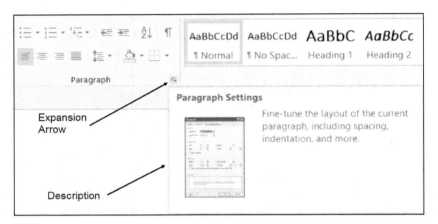

DIALOGUE BOX

Dialogue boxes are pop-up boxes that cover specialized settings. As just mentioned, if you click on an expansion arrow, it will often open a dialogue box that contains more choices than are visible in that section. When you right-click in a Word document and choose Font, Paragraph, or Hyperlink that also opens dialogue boxes. Dialogue boxes allow the most granular level of control over an option

This is the Replace dialogue box.

This may not apply to you, but be aware that if you have more than one Word document open and open a dialogue box in one of those documents, you may not be able to move to the other documents you have open until you close the dialogue box.

SCROLL BAR

This is more useful in Excel than in Word, but on the right-hand side of the screen you should see a scroll bar. You can either click in the space above or below the bar to move up or down a small amount or you can left-click on the bar, hold the left-click, and drag the bar up or down to move through the document more quickly. You can also use the arrows at the top and the bottom to move up and down through your document. (The scroll bar isn't always visible in Word. If you don't see it, move your mouse over to the side of the screen and it should appear.)

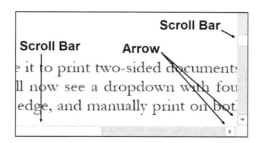

In general, you shouldn't see a scroll bar at the bottom of the screen, but it is possible. This would happen if you ever change the zoom level of your document to the point that you're not seeing the entire width of the document in a single screen. (Not something I recommend when working with normal documents.)

ARROW

If I ever tell you to arrow to the left or right or up or down, that just means use your arrow keys. This will move your cursor to the left one space, to the right one space, up one line, or down one line. If you're at the end of a line and arrow to the right, it will take you to the beginning of the next line. If you're at the beginning of a line and arrow to the left, it will take you to the end of the last line.

CURSOR

There are two possible meanings for cursor. One is the one I just used. In your Word document, you will see that there is a blinking line. This indicates where you are in the document. If you type text, each letter will appear where the cursor was at the time you typed it. The cursor will move (at least in the U.S. and I'd assume most European versions) to the right as you type. This version of the cursor should be visible at all times unless you have text selected.

The other type of cursor is the one that's tied to the movement of your mouse or trackpad. When you're typing, it will not be visible. But stop typing and move your mouse or trackpad, and you'll see it. If the cursor is positioned over your text, it will look somewhat like a tall skinny capital I. If you move it up to the menu options or off to the sides, it becomes a white arrow. (Except for when you position it over any option under the tabs that can be typed in such as Font Size or Font where it will once again look like a skinny capital I.)

Usually I won't refer to your cursor, I'll just say, "click" or "select" or whatever action you need to take with it, but moving the cursor to that location will be implied.

QUICK ACCESS TOOLBAR

You might notice that the options in the very top left corner of my version of Word are different from what you see. That's because I've customized the Quick Access Toolbar. You can do this on your version of Word by clicking on the arrow you see at the very end of the list and then checking the commands you want to have available there. It can be useful if there's something you're doing repeatedly (like inserting section breaks) that's located on a different tab than something else you're doing repeatedly (like formatting text).

Of course, it's only useful if you use it. Half the time I forget I've done that. But if you can remember, it's a nice time-saver.

CONTROL SHORTCUTS

Throughout this document, I'm going to mention various control shortcuts that you can use to perform tasks like save, copy, cut, and paste. (There's a list of the most important ones in the appendix.) Each of these will be written as Ctrl + a capital letter, but when you use the shortcut on your computer you don't need to use the capitalized version of the letter. For example, holding down the Ctrl key and the s key at the same time will save your document. I'll write this as Ctrl + S, but that just means hold down the key that says ctrl and the s key at the same time.

ABSOLUTE BASICS

Before we do anything else, there are a few absolute basics that we should cover.

STARTING A NEW WORD FILE

To start a brand new Word file, I click on Word 2013 from my applications menu or the shortcut I have on my computer's taskbar. If you're already in Word and want to open a new Word file, go to the File tab and choose New from the left-hand menu.

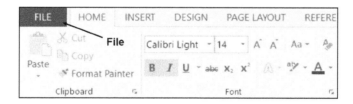

Whichever option you choose will bring up a list of various templates, including the first option which is for a "Blank document". Ninety-nine percent of the time that's the one you'll want. To use it, left-click on the image.

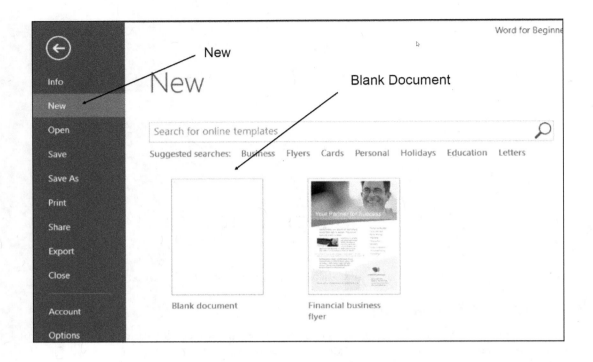

OPENING AN EXISTING WORD FILE

To open an existing Word file you can either go to the folder where the file is saved and double-click on the file name, or (if Word is already open) go to the File tab and choose Open from the left-hand menu. Or you can just open Word without selecting a file and it will provide a list of recent documents to choose from on the left-hand side.

If you're in Word and the document you need is listed, left-click on it once and it will open as long as you haven't renamed the file or moved it since it was last open. (In that case, you'll need to navigate to where the file is saved and open it that way, either through Word or outside of Word.)

To navigate to the file you need, click on Open Other Documents and then click on Computer under Open (if you just opened Word and don't have any files open) or click on Computer under Home (if you already had a file open).

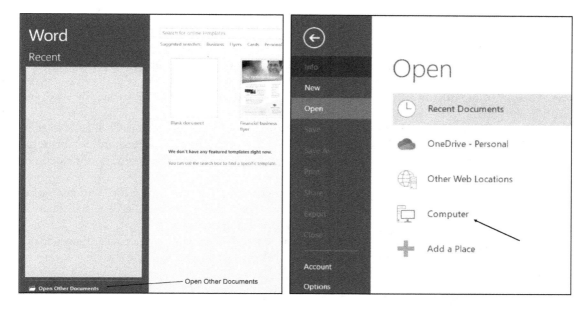

This should give you a list of recent folders you've used or you can click on Browse if the file you need isn't in one of those folders. When you click on Browse this will bring up the Open dialogue box (below). From there you can navigate to any location on your computer.

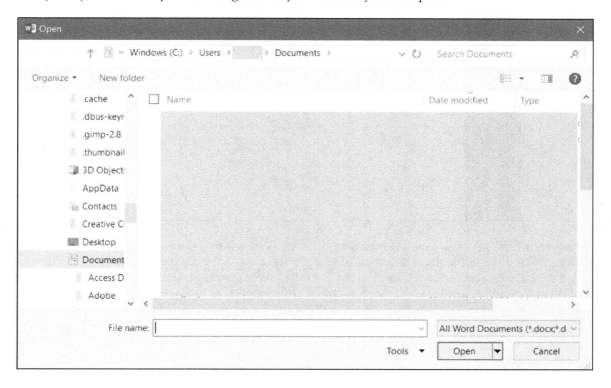

SAVING A WORD FILE

To quickly save a document, you can use Ctrl + S or click on the small image of a floppy disk in the top left corner of the screen above File. For a document you've already saved that will overwrite the prior version of the document with the current version and will keep the file name, file type, and file location the same.

If you try to save a file that has never been saved before, it will automatically default to the Save As option which requires that you specify where to save the file, give it a name, and designate the file type. There are defaults for name and format, but you'll want to change the name of the document to something better than Document2.

You can also choose Save As when you want to change the location of a file, the name of a file, or the file type. (With respect to file type, I sometimes need to, for example, save a .doc file as a .pdf file or a .doc file as a .docx file for use with certain formatting programs.)

The first choice you have to make for Save As is where you want to save the file. I see a list of my most recent six folders listed and can also choose to Browse if I want to use a different location than one of the folders listed.

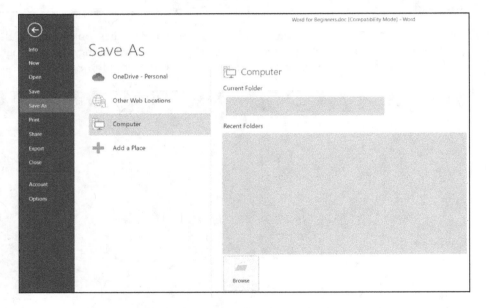

When you click on the location where you want to save the file, this will bring up the Save As dialogue box. Type in the name you want for the file and choose the file type. My file type defaults to Word 97-2003 Document (.doc) which is the format I prefer to save in because it's the easiest format for all users and all versions of Word to open. If you save as a .docx file you may encounter situations where someone you share the file with won't be able to open it.

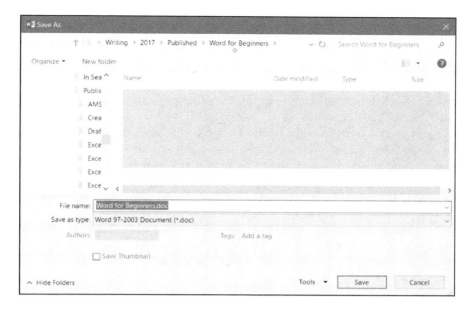

If you had already saved the file and you choose to Save As but keep the same location, name, and format as before, Word will overwrite the previous version of the file just like it would have if you'd used Save.

If you just want to rename a file, it's actually best to close the file and then go to where the file is saved and rename it that way rather than use Save As. Using Save As will keep the original of the file as well as creating the newer version. That's great when you want version control (which I often need), but not when you just wanted to rename your file from Great Book Version 22 to Great Book FINAL.

RENAMING A WORD FILE

As discussed above, you can use Save As to give an existing file a new name, but that approach will leave you with two versions of the file, one with the old name and one with the new name. If you just want to change the name of the existing file, close it and then navigate to where you've saved it. Click on the file name once to select it, click on it a second time to highlight the name, and then type in the new name you want to use, replacing the old one. If you rename the file this way outside of Word, there will only be one version of the file left, the one with the new name you wanted.

Just be aware that if you rename a file by navigating to where it's located and changing the name you won't be able to access the file from the Recent Workbooks listing under Open file, since that will still list the old name which no longer exists.

DELETING A WORD FILE

You can't delete a Word file from within Word. You need to close the file you want to delete and then navigate to where the file is stored and delete the file there without opening it. Once you've located the file, click on the file name. (Only enough to select it. Make sure you haven't double-clicked and highlighted the name which will delete the file name but not the file.) Next, choose

Delete from the menu at the top of the screen, or right-click and choose Delete from the dropdown menu.

CLOSING A WORD FILE

To close a Word file click on the X in the top right corner or go to File and then choose Close. (You can also use Ctrl + W, but I never have.)

If no changes have been made to the document since you saved it last, it will just close.

If changes have been made, Word should ask you if you want to save those changes. You can either choose to save them, not save them, or cancel closing the document and leave it open. I almost always default to saving any changes. If I'm in doubt about whether I'd be overwriting something important, I cancel and choose to Save As and save the current file as a later version of the document just in case (e.g., Great Book v2).

If you had copied an image or a large block of text, you may also have a box pop up asking if you want to keep that image or text when you close the document. Usually the answer to this is no, but if you had planned on pasting that image or text somewhere else and hadn't yet done so, you can say to keep it on the clipboard.

BASIC TASKS

At its most basic, adding text into a Word document is incredibly simple. You simply open a new document and start typing. When you're done, you save the document.

Go ahead and do it. See? Open. Type. Save. Voila.

But you probably want to do more with your text than that. And we'll cover all the formatting, which is the majority of what you'll want to do, in the next section. First, I want to cover a few basic functions that you can perform in Word that will make your life easier as you enter your text and then edit it.

UNDO

Undo lets you take the last thing (or few things) you did, and undo it. That means you don't have to be afraid to try something that you're not sure will work, because you can always reverse it.

To undo something, simply type Ctrl + Z. If you did a few things you didn't like, just keep typing Ctrl + Z until they're all gone. But beware that Word undoes things in order, so if you want to undo the second-to-last thing you did, you'll have to first undo the last thing you did.

REDO

If you take it too far and undo too much and want something back, then you can choose to redo. That's done by typing Ctrl + Y. Go ahead and try it out. Type a sentence in your document. Undo it with Ctrl + Z and then redo it with Ctrl + Y. Easy peasy.

(If you don't want to use control keys, you can also add undo and redo to the Quick Access Toolbar, but I'd highly recommend that you memorize these two. You'll work much faster if you can memorize the control key shortcuts for undo, redo, save, copy, cut, and paste.)

DELETE

Another basic task you need to master is how to delete text. There are a few ways to do this. If you're trying to delete something that you just typed, use the backspace key to delete the letters one at a time.

You can also place the cursor next to the text you want to delete and then use the backspace or delete keys, depending on where the cursor is relative to the text you're trying to delete. If your cursor is on the left-hand side of text, use the delete key. On the right-hand side, use the backspace key. (And if you get it wrong, remember that you have Ctrl + Z to undo what you just did.)

If you want to delete a large chunk of text at one time, select the text you want to delete and then use the delete OR backspace key.

SELECT ALL

The other basic task that you should know about before we start talking formatting is how to select all of the text in your document.

Select All is very useful for applying a format to your entire document. I tend to write in the default font that Word uses and then change the font once I'm done. It's also handy if you want to copy the contents of one document into another. Say, for example, you worked on a group project and each person wrote their individual piece in a separate document and now you need to combine them. Or, like me, you wrote your first novel using separate files for each chapter (Don't do that, by the way.) You can take those final documents, select all, copy, and paste into one master document that combines them.

To Select All, go to the Home tab and then to the Editing section on the far right-hand side and click on the arrow next to Select. In the dropdown menu choose Select All.

Another option is to use Ctrl + A, although I don't consider this one of the control shortcuts that I use often enough to memorize.

I've also added Select All as one of my Quick Access Toolbar options.

If you ever choose all of the text in a document and then decide you didn't want to, just click somewhere in the document and the selection will go away. (You can also arrow up or down, but that will take you to the top or the bottom of the document and you may not want that.)

COPYING, CUTTING, AND PASTING

Copy and Cut are similar. They're both a way to move text from one location to another. Copy leaves the text where it was and creates a copy of that text to move to the new location. Cut removes the text from where it was and puts the text on a "clipboard" (that's usually not visible to you) for movement to a new location.

Paste is how you tell Word where that new location is.

The first step in copying or cutting text is to select all of the text you want to move. To select text you can left-click on one side of the text, hold down that left-click and move your mouse or trackpad until all of the text you want is highlighted. Or you can use the shift key and the arrow keys to select your text.

Once your text is selected, to copy it type Ctrl + C or to cut it type Ctrl + X.

If you don't want to use the control shortcuts, you can also go to the Home tab and in the Clipboard section choose Copy or Cut from there. Or you can right-click after you've selected your text and choose Copy or Cut from the dropdown menu.

I recommend using the control shortcuts, because it's the fastest and these three commands are ones you'll use often enough to make it worth memorizing them.

If you copy text, it remains visible in the location you copied it from. Behind the scenes Word has taken a copy of that text and placed it on a "clipboard" for use elsewhere.

If you cut text, the text is immediately removed from the document. It too is placed on a "clipboard" for use elsewhere. (This also means that cut text, if you choose not to paste it somewhere else, is deleted text.)

To see the clipboard where the items you've copied or cut are stored, go to the Home tab and click on the expansion arrow next to Clipboard. This will bring up a Clipboard display with all of the items you've recently copied or cut from your document.

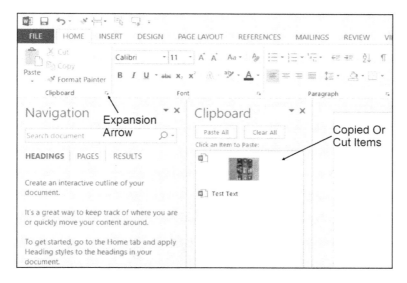

As you can see here, I copied two snippets of text as well as took a screenshot. I could use this clipboard to paste all of those items into my document at once using that Paste All option. (This wasn't always an available option in Word so if you have a really old version you won't be able to see or do this.)

You can also just click on one of the items and it will paste into your document. This can come in handy if you have something you need to paste more than once into your document, but usually you won't need this. You'll just want to copy or cut one item and then paste it into another spot in your document (or another document) right then.

The simplest way to paste something you've just copied or cut is to use Ctrl + V. Simply copy or cut your item, go to where you want to place it, type Ctrl + V, and you're done.

Your other two options are to go to the Clipboard section of the Home tab and click on Paste. Or you can right-click and choose one of the Paste options from the dropdown menu in the document.

PASTE OPTIONS

If you use Ctrl + V to paste text, you'll be pasting not only the text you copied or cut, but its formatting as well. Usually, that's fine and you'll probably be able to use Ctrl + V ninety-five percent of the time. (And even if you don't want to keep the formatting, there's a trick I'll show you later—using the Format Painter—that you can use to quickly correct formatting after you paste the text into its new location. All it requires is that you have some text that's already formatted the way you want.)

But sometimes you'll want to paste the text in without that formatting. That's where using the Paste dropdown menus comes in handy, because they allow you to choose how you paste your item.

As you can see in the images above, once you've copied or cut an item, you'll be given three paste options: Keep Source Formatting, Merge Formatting, and Keep Text Only. (They're represented by small images, but if you hold your mouse over each one, you'll be able to see the labels.)

In the image below I've pasted the red and bolded word TEST written in Calibri font into a sentence written in black font in Times New Roman using each paste option. This shows how text in a different color, font, and bolding is handled under each paste option.

> **TEST**
>
> Ctrl + V (Paste)
>
> Sample **TEST** text for demonstration purposes.
>
> Keep Source Formatting
>
> Sample **TEST** text for demonstration purposes.
>
> Merge Formatting
>
> Sample **TEST** text for demonstration purposes.
>
> Keep Text Only
>
> Sample TEST text for demonstration purposes.

Using Ctrl + V, the color, font, and bolding of the original text remain.

Using Keep Source Formatting gives the same result. Color, font, and bolding are the same as the original text.

With Merge Formatting the color and font of the original text are lost, but the bolding of the original text is not. So "TEST" is now in Times New Roman and black, but it's still bolded.

Using Keep Text Only the color, font, and bolding of the original text are all lost and replaced with the color, font, and bolding (in this case none) of the destination text.

That may seem a little confusing, and honestly, my recommendation is to just use Ctrl + V and fix the formatting after the text is in your document. The main time I use these other paste options is when copying from websites that use hyperlinks that I don't want to bring into my document. Then I paste using Keep Text Only.

If you remember anything from what we just walked through, remember this:

Ctrl + C to copy.

Ctrl + X to cut.

Ctrl + V to paste.

TEXT FORMATTING

Now that you know how to create a file, enter the text you want, and save your work, it's time to actually format that text. Let's start with font.

CHOOSING A FONT – GENERAL THOUGHTS

The font you use governs the general appearance of the text in your document. My version of Word uses Calibri font as the default, but there are hundreds of fonts you can choose. Here is a sample of a few of those choices:

Sans-Serif Examples:

Calibri

Arial

Gill Sans MT

Serif Font Examples:

Times New Roman

Garamond

Palatino Linotype

The first three samples are sans-serif fonts. (That just means they don't have little feet at the bottom of the letters.) The second three samples are serif fonts. (They do have those little feet at the bottom of each letter.) All of these fonts are the same size, but you can see that the different fonts have a different appearance and take up different amounts of space on the page. Arial is darker and taller than Calibri, for example.

Many companies and teachers will specify the font you need to use. If they don't I'd suggest using a serifed font like Garamond or Times New Roman for text since serifed fonts are supposed to be easier to read.

And unless you're working on a creative project, don't get too fancy with your fonts. The six listed in that example above should cover almost any text needs you have. At the end of the day, the goal is for someone to be able to read what you've written. So no Algerian in many body text. Save those fonts for embellishments and section labels.

CHANGING THE FONT

There are a few ways you can change the font in your document. If you already know you want to use a different font, it's easiest to do so before you start typing. Otherwise you'll need to select all of the text you want to change. (Either with Select All if it's all text in the document or by selecting chunks of text and changing them one chunk at a time.)

The first way to change the font is to go to the Font section of the Home tab. Click on the arrow to the right of the current font name and choose from the dropdown menu.

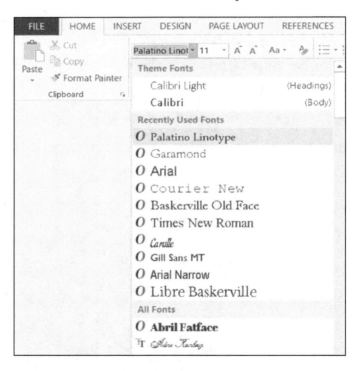

The first section of the dropdown menu lists the fonts for the theme you're using. Usually that'll be the defaults for Word, in this case, Calibri and Calibri Light. Next you'll see Recently Used Fonts. Most of the time there will only be one or two fonts here, but I had used a number recently.

Finally, you'll see a list of all available fonts in alphabetical order. If you know the font you want, you can start typing in its name rather than scroll through the entire list. Otherwise, use the scroll bar on the right-hand side to move through the list. Each font is written using the font to give you an idea what it will look like. See in the example the difference between Algerian and Garamond?

The next way to change your font is to right-click and choose Font from the dropdown menu. This will bring up the Font dialogue box. In the top left corner you can choose the font you want.

There's a third option for changing the font, something I'm going to call the mini formatting menu, in the newest versions of Word. To see this menu, right-click in your document or select a section of text using your mouse. When you select a section of text, a smaller version of the Font section of the Home tab will appear just above your text. If you right-click it will appear above the dropdown menu.

As you can see, one of the options that you can change in the mini formatting menu is the font. (If the font name box is empty, that's because you have text selected and there's more than one font in the selection.) To change the font, click on the arrow to the right of the listed font and choose the one you want from the dropdown just like you would in the Font section of the Home tab. I would recommend that you only use this option for a selection of text that you want to change to a new font. It's much better to change the font for your document in the Home tab.

FONT SIZE

Font size dictates how large the text will be. Here are some examples of different font sizes:

8 pt   12 pt   16 pt

As you can see, the larger the font size, the larger the text. Most documents are written in a ten, eleven, or twelve point font size. Often footnotes or endnotes will use eight or nine point. Chapter headings or title pages will use the larger font sizes. Whatever font size you do use, try to be consistent between different sections of your document. So all main body text should use just one font size. Same for chapter or section headings.

Changing the font size works much the same way as changing the font. You have the same three options: You can go to the Font section of the Home tab, bring up the mini formatting menu by right-clicking, or bring up the Font dialogue box by right-clicking and choosing Font from the dropdown menu. If you want to change existing text, you need to select the text first. If you want to change the font size for text that you're going to type, do so with the Home tab or the Font dialogue box options.

For all three options the font size is listed to the right of the font name.

For the Home tab or mini formatting menu options, you can click on the arrow next to the current font size to bring up a dropdown menu that lets you choose your font size. In the Font dialogue box that list of choices is already visible.

If the font size you want isn't listed, you can type it in instead. Just click into the box for font size and change the number to the font size you want to use.

In the Home tab and the mini formatting menu, if you're only changing the font by one or two point sizes, you can instead use the increase and decrease font options directly to the right of the font size. These are depicted as the letter A with a small arrow above it. The one on the left is an arrow that points upward (to increase the font size). The one on the right is an arrow that points downward (to decrease the font size). If you use the increase/decrease font options, they increase and decrease the font size one place according to the font sizes listed in the dropdown menu.

Here is an image of all three choices for changing font size in the Home tab.

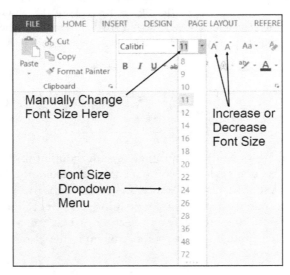

FONT COLOR

Changing your font color works the same as changing your font or font size. Select the text you want to change and then either go to the Font section of the Home tab, pull up the mini formatting menu, or right-click and choose Font from the dropdown menu to bring up the Font dialogue box. This time, though, you want to click on the arrow next to the A with the solid colored line under it in the bottom right corner of the section:

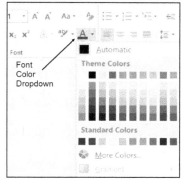

This will give you a dropdown menu with seventy different colors to choose from. Click on the color you want and it will change your text to that color.

If those seventy choices are not enough, you can click on More Colors at the bottom of the dropdown box. This will bring up the Colors dialogue box where you can choose from even more colors or specify a specific color in the Custom tab using RGB values. (Not likely to be needed for a font color, but this does come into play for fill color and is discussed in more detail in *Intermediate Word*.)

HIGHLIGHTING TEXT

Another thing you can do is highlight text in a document much like you might do with a highlighter. You can do this from the Font section of the Home tab or in the mini formatting menu. Select the text you want to highlight and then look for the letters ab and what looks like a pen running diagonally right to left between the ab and a colored line:

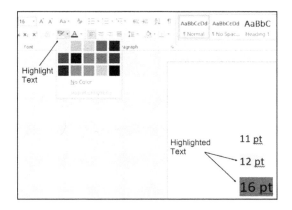

If you want to highlight using the color shown in the line, you can just click on the image. If you want to use a different color, left-click on the arrow and select your color from the dropdown menu.

If you ever highlight text and want to remove the highlight, you can do so by selecting that text, going to the highlight dropdown, and choosing the "no color" option.

Once you've used the highlighter it will show the last color you used as the default color until you close the file. (This carries across documents. I have three documents open at the moment and all three of them now show "no color" as the highlighter option even though I only used it in the one document.)

BOLDING TEXT

This is one you will use often. At least I do. The easiest way to bold text is to use Ctrl + B. You can use it before you start typing the text you want to bold or on a selection of text that you've chosen. For text that is already bolded, you can remove the bolding by selecting the text and using Ctrl + B as well. If you select text that is both bolded and not bolded, you'll need to type Ctrl + B twice, once to bold all of the text and once to remove it.

If you don't want to use the control keys, you can also go to the Font Section of the Home tab and click on the B on the left-hand side. It works the exact same way as using Ctrl + B. If you click on it and then type text that text will be bolded. Or you can select the text you want to bold and then click on the B. To turn off or remove bolding, click on the B again.

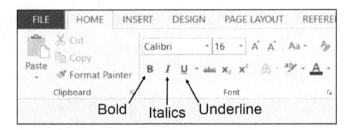

The final option is to select your text, right-click, choose Font from the dropdown menu, and then choose to Bold in the Font Style section of the Font dialogue box. (If you want to both bold and italicize text, you would choose Bold Italic.)

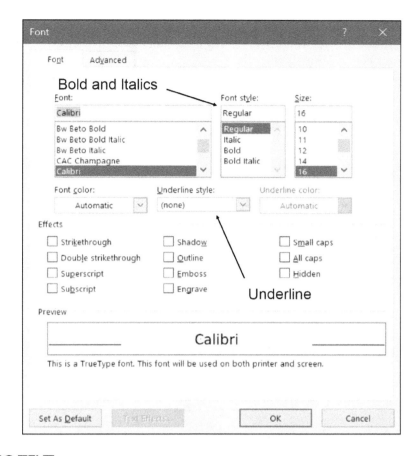

ITALICIZING TEXT

To place text into italics—that means to have it sloped to the side *like this*—the easiest way is to use Ctrl + I. It works the exact same way as bolding text. You can do it before you type the letters or select the text and then use it. And to remove italics, just select the text, and then type Ctrl + I until the italics are gone.

Or in the Font section of the Home tab, you can click on the slanted capital I. And if you use the Font dialogue box, italics are listed under Font Styles. (See the images above in the Bolding section.)

UNDERLINING TEXT

Underlining text works much the same way as bolding or italicizing text. The control keys you'll need to use are Ctrl + U and in the Font section of the Home tab the underline option is represented by an underlined U. (See image above in the Bolding section.)

Underline is different from italics and bold, though, because there are multiple underline options to choose from. Using Ctrl + U will provide a single line underline of your text. So will just clicking on the U in the Font section of the Home tab.

But if you click on the arrow next to the U in the Font section, you will see seven additional underline options you can choose from.

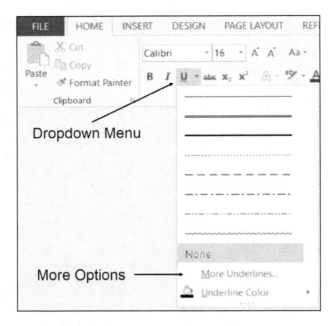

Choosing More Underlines at the bottom of that list of options will open the Font dialogue box where you will have a total of seventeen underline styles to choose from. You can also go direct to the Font dialogue box by selecting your text and then right-clicking and choosing Font from the dropdown. But, honestly, while it's good to know those other options are there the basic single underline will be all you need most of the time so if you remember anything remember Ctrl +U.

REMOVING BOLDING, UNDERLINING, OR ITALICS

I touched on this briefly above, but let's go over it again.

If you have bolded, underlined, or italicized text and you want to remove that formatting, you can simply select the text and use the command in question to remove that formatting type. So Ctrl + B, I, or U or click on the letter in the Font section of the Home tab or go to the Font dialogue box and remove the formatting from there.

If you select text that is partially formatted one way and partially formatted another—so say half of it is bolded and half is not—you may need to use the command twice. The first time will apply the formatting to all of the selected text, the second time will remove it from all of the selected text.

Also, with specialty underlining (all but the default, first choice), using Ctrl + U once will revert the type of underlining to the basic single underline. To remove the underline altogether, you'll need to use Ctrl + U a second time.

COPYING FORMATTING

There are going to be times where you've already formatted part of your document or you have a document that's formatted in the way you want and you want to "copy" that formatting to another portion of your document or a different document. This is where the Format Painter tool comes in handy. It's located on the Home tab in the Clipboard section.

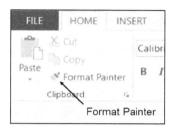

We have yet to discuss formatting paragraphs, but it's really useful when it comes to that because it will copy not only basic formatting like the font, font size, color, bolding, underline, italics, etc. but also the paragraph spacing and indent. Often in my corporate career I was able to use the format painter to fix a document when nothing else worked.

If you want to take formatting from one set of text and use it on another, first select the text with the formatting you want. Next, click on the Format Painter image. Finally, select the text you want to copy the formatting to.

A few tips.

You need to use the mouse or trackpad to select the text you want to have the formatting. Using the arrow and shift keys doesn't work.

You'll know that the format painter is ready to paint the format when you see a little paintbrush next to your cursor as you hover over your document.

You can sweep formatting that's in one document to another document.

Format painting can be unreliable if there are different formats in the sample you're taking the formatting from. For example, if I have a sample where part of the text is red and part of the text is bolded and I format sweep from that sample to new text, only the formatting of the first letter in my sample will carry over.

Sometimes with paragraph or numbered list formatting, I have to select the paragraph from the bottom to the top instead of top to bottom in order to get the format painter to carry over the formatting I want. And sometimes I need to select more than one paragraph to sweep from in order to get the line spacing to carry over.

Last but not least, when you copy formatting over, all of the formatting in your target text will be removed. This can be an issue if you've used italics or bolding within a paragraph, for example. Maybe you want the paragraph spacing and font and font size from another document so you use the format painter. Problem is, any bold, italics, or underline in the text you're copying the formatting to will be lost.

We'll talk about how to do this later, but there is a way in newer versions of Word to find all italicized text in a document. Same with bolded or underlined. So you could format sweep and then go back to a prior version of the document, locate the italics, bolding, and underlining, and manually put them back into the document now that it has the new formatting. It all depends on which option will be easier.

In summary, while the format painter is incredibly powerful and I use it all the time, you also need to be cautious in how you apply it so that you don't inadvertently introduce errors or erase formatting you don't want to erase. Sometimes it's the only way I can get paragraphs to look the same. Nothing else will do it. So learn this tool. It *will* save you at some point or another.

PARAGRAPH FORMATTING

That was basic text formatting. Now it's time to cover paragraph formatting. This is where you set the indent for a paragraph or make sure that it's double-spaced or that there's enough separation between paragraphs.

In this guide we're going to walk through how to change the formatting of a specific paragraph. Once you're comfortable enough in Word, I'd advise that you learn Styles and use those instead. We're not going to cover them in this guide because to really use them well you need to create customized Styles which is beyond a beginner-level skill. I will touch on a few points about Styles at the end of this chapter, though, and they are covered in *Intermediate Word* if you reach the point you want to learn about them. (Also, at the end of this guide I'll point you towards other resources you can use to learn what isn't covered here.)

Alright then. Let's talk about how to format a paragraph one element at a time.

PARAGRAPH ALIGNMENT

There are four choices for paragraph alignment. Left, Center, Right, and Justified. In the image below I've taken the same three-line paragraph and applied each alignment style to it:

This paragraph is **left-aligned**. I now need to add enough text to this paragraph to make more than one line so you can see the difference between the different alignments. Good times. Especially since I need at least three lines each for you to really see this.

This paragraph is **centered**. I now need to add enough text to this paragraph to make more than one line so you can see the difference between the different alignments. Good times. Especially since I need at least three lines each for you to really see this.

This paragraph is **right-aligned**. I now need to add enough text to this paragraph to make more than one line so you can see the difference between the different alignments. Good times. Especially since I need at least three lines each for you to really see this.

This paragraph is **justified**. I now need to add enough text to this paragraph to make more than one line so you can see the difference between the different alignments. Good times. Especially since I need at least three lines each for you to really see this.

Left-aligned, the first example, is how you'll often see text in documents. The text is lined up along the left-hand side of the page and allowed to end in a jagged line on the right-hand side of the page.

Justified, the last example, is the other common way for text to be presented. Text is still aligned along the left-hand side, but instead of leaving the right-hand side ragged, Word adjusts the spacing between words so that all lines are also aligned along the right-hand side.

For school papers and most work documents you're probably going to use left-alignment. Some places may prefer justified. Books are often published with justified but many do use left-aligned.

Centered, the second example, is rarely used for full paragraphs of text like the main body text of a book. It can be used for sections of text that are only a few lines long such as a quote that starts a chapter. Also, it's often used for chapter or section titles that are then centered over left-aligned or justified text. As you can see, it centers each line and distributes the text for that line equally to the left and right of the center point.

Right-aligned, the third example, is rare. It aligns all of the text along the right-hand side and leaves the left-hand side ragged. I have seen it used for text in side margins of non-fiction books and would expect to see it used for languages that read right to left.

Now that you understand the difference between the options, how do you change the paragraph alignment of your text? As with font, you can do this either before you start typing or by selecting text you've already typed. (For just one paragraph, you can click anywhere in the paragraph, you don't need to select the whole paragraph.)

The way I change paragraph alignment is by going to the Paragraph section of the Home tab and clicking on the image for the alignment type I need in the bottom row of that section.

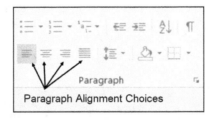

Paragraph Alignment Choices

Each image contains lines that show that type of alignment, but you can also hold your mouse over each one and Word will tell you which one it is.

There are also control shortcuts. Ctrl + L will left-align, Ctrl + E will center your text, Ctrl + R will right-align, and Ctrl + J will justify it. The only one of these I use enough to have memorized is Ctrl + E. I either use left-alignment, which is the default, or I use a Style that includes justifying the text. Since centering is something you do with section headers, I do use that one fairly often.

The third way to change your paragraph alignment is to right-click in your document and choose Paragraph from the dropdown menu. This will give you the Paragraph dialogue box. The first option within that box is a dropdown where you can choose the alignment type you want.

PARAGRAPH SPACING

If you've ever attended school in the United States, you've probably been told at some point to submit a five-page paper that's double-spaced with one inch margins. Or if you've ever submitted a short story you were told to use a specific line spacing. So how do you do that?

As with the other formatting options, you can either do this before you start typing or by selecting the paragraphs you want to change after they've been entered into the document.

Once you're ready, go to the Paragraph section of the Home tab and locate the Line and Paragraph Spacing option. It's to the right of the paragraph alignment options and looks like five lines of text with two big blue arrows on the left-hand side, one pointing up, one pointing down. Click on the small black arrow to the right of the image to bring up the dropdown menu.

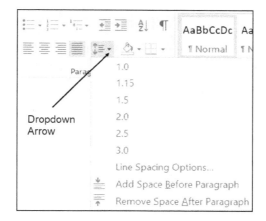

You'll see that you have a choice of single-spaced (1.0) or double-spaced (2.0) as well as 1.15, 1.5, 2.5, and 3.0 spacing. If you want a different spacing than one of those options, then click on Line Spacing Options at the bottom of the list to bring up the Paragraph dialogue box. There you can enter an exact number or choose from even more options. Generally, the dropdown will be sufficient, though.

Another option, of course, is to just go straight to the Paragraph dialogue box by right-clicking and choosing Paragraph from the dropdown menu. (Just remember to have already selected the text you want to change or to change the spacing before you start typing.)

BULLETED LISTS

A bulleted list is just what it sounds like, a list of items where each line starts with a bullet mark on the left-hand side. The most common bullet choice is probably a small dark black circle that's filled in, but Word has a few options you can choose from:

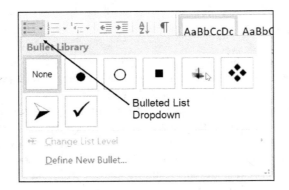

To create a bulleted list, go to the Paragraph section of the Home tab and click on the bulleted list dropdown menu to select the type of bullet you want to use in your list.

If you know that what you're about to type is going to be a bulleted list, you can click on the bulleted list option before you start typing. Word will insert the bullet you've chosen and move the cursor to where your text will start.

If you've already typed the first row of text that you want bulleted, you can click on the bulleted list option you want while in that row of text and it will convert it to the first entry of a bulleted list.

Hitting enter at the end of the line in a bulleted list, will start a new line with a bullet.

Or, last but not least, if all of your text has already been entered you can select all of the lines that you want to be part of the bulleted list and then choose the bulleted list option and it should convert your text to a bulleted list with one bullet per paragraph or individual line.

If you have a line that's bulleted and you don't want it to be, you can go to the beginning of the text on that line and backspace. Once will remove the bullet. Twice will move the text to the beginning of the line. Or, you can select the line and choose None from the bulleted list dropdown menu.

(You can also use the Format Painter to apply bullets to a list of entries or to remove them depending on the formatting of your source data.)

Another way to create a bulleted list is to select your text and then right-click to bring up the mini formatting menu. The bulleted list dropdown is one of the available options.

With bulleted lists, Word automatically indents your text. If you don't want that, you can use the Decrease Indent option (discussed below) to move the text back to the left-hand side of the page but keep the bullets.

NUMBERED LISTS

You can also create a "numbered" list that uses letters or numbers for each entry in your list instead of bullets.

One easy way to create a numbered list in more recent versions of Word is to simply type the first number you want to use, the separator mark you want, and then a space. Word will automatically indent that entry and turn it into the first entry in a numbered list. So, for example, I might type the number 1 followed by a period and then a space. Word will indent that 1. and make it the first entry in my list. This works with all of the options on the dropdown menu we're about to look at. (This is part of the Autocorrect settings, so a little thunderbolt will appear next to the number when this first happens. If you don't want that to happen, you can click on the arrow next to the thunderbolt and have Word reverse the change by telling it to Undo Automatic Numbering.)

When you hit enter after typing in the text for your first line, Word will continue the numbering you started.

The other option, especially if you already have your list and just need to convert it to a numbered list, is to select the lines you want to number, go to the Home tab and in the Paragraph section click on the arrow next to the Numbering option and choose the numbered list option you want from there.

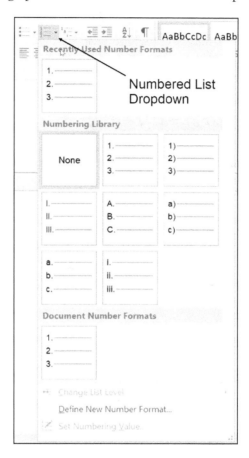

As you can see, you have the option to choose between lists that use 1, 2, 3 or i, ii, iii or A, B, C or a, b, c, or I, II, III and then between using a period after the "number" or a paren. For a basic list, this should be all you really need.

When you right-click on your list you'll also see that the mini formatting menu is available and that one of the options is the numbering option. So instead of going to the Home tab, you could just right-click and choose from there to create your numbered list.

You can also create two-level or three-level lists by using the tab key to indent your numbering or the shift-tab key to decrease the indent on your numbering. This gives you, for example, a first level that is 1, 2, 3 with the option of a second level under that that's a, b, c. To do this, go to each line you want to be second-level (or third-level) and use the tab key to indent that line. This will change the numbering of the line at the same time it moves it inward.

If you need very fine control over a multi-level list or you need a list that works throughout your document and has lots of breaks in it, you'll probably want to use an option we're not going to cover here called the Multilevel List option. (It's the option to the right of the number list option in the Paragraph section.) I discuss that option in *Intermediate Word*, but I'll tell you now that it's incredibly finicky to use and one of the things I hate most in Word.

Back to basic numbered lists. If you had a numbered list earlier in your document and want that numbering to continue in the location where you are now, you can do that. Or, if Word continued the numbering and you wanted it to start over at 1, you can do that, too. In either case, you're going to right-click on the number you want to change. You'll then either choose Continue Numbering (to continue from a prior section) or Set Numbering Value (to change the value you start with back to 1 or A or whatever you're using).

INDENTING AN ENTIRE PARAGRAPH OR LIST

Now that we've talked about lists, let's talk about increasing or decreasing an indent. When you're dealing with paragraphs, the best way to do this is in the Paragraph dialogue box. Right-click on your paragraph and from the dropdown menu choose Paragraph. Once the Paragraph dialogue box opens, you can set the indent for the entire paragraph as well as whether the paragraph will have a special indent only for the first line.

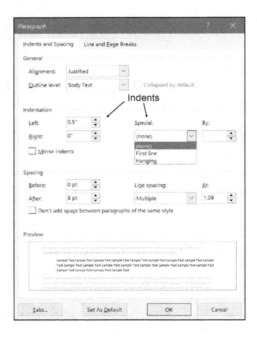

To indent the entire paragraph, change the value under Indentation where it says Left. To indent just the first line of a paragraph, choose First Line from the dropdown menu under Special and then select by how much in the By box. To have the first line flush left, but the lines below that indented, choose Hanging from the dropdown menu under Special and then selected how much those other lines should be indented by entering a value in the By box. (Usually .3 is a good value to go with, Word defaults to .5)

If you just want to indent a line of text or an entire paragraph, you can use the Increase Indent (or Decrease Indent) options in the Paragraph section of the Home tab. These are the ones that have four lines with blue arrows pointing either to the left (for decrease indent) or the right (for increase indent). You can also use tab (to indent) and shift + tab (to decrease an indent).

The problem with the increase indent/decrease indent menu options or the tab keys is in how Word records this for your paragraph format. For example, I just took a single word and indented it using the tab key. Word interpreted this as me wanting that paragraph to be formatted as having a First Line indent of .5". When I instead used the increase indent option on that single word of text, Word interpreted it as Left Indentation of .5". If it's just one line of text, it doesn't matter. But when you're dealing with an entire document, these little discrepancies can become a nightmare.

For bulleted and numbered lists, if you want to move an entire list further to the right or further to the left, select the entire list and then use either the Paragraph dialogue box, the shift or shift + tab keys, or the increase or decrease indent options from the Paragraph section of the Home tab to move it. The Paragraph dialogue box will give you the most control. The tab and shift + tab keys are probably the easiest to use. You can also right-click and choose Adjust Line Indents.

(If you choose Adjust Line Indents, you can also adjust the space between the number and the text by changing the Follow Number With option. This can be very useful when you have a numbered list that gets into the double digits.)

SPACING BETWEEN PARAGRAPHS

If you choose to style your paragraphs as left-aligned with no first line indent, you're going to need space between your paragraphs. The default style in Word is set up this way. You'll see that as you hit enter for a new paragraph that there's space left between the old paragraph and the new one.

If that space isn't present, you may be tempted to create one by using the enter key. Don't. It will mess with your formatting in a larger document as those spaces you've entered end up at the top or bottom of your pages. It's better to instead format your paragraphs to include the space.

You can do this by selecting your paragraph(s) and going to the Paragraph section of the Home tab. Click on the arrow next to the Line and Paragraph Spacing image (the lines with two blue arrows on the left-hand side, one pointing upward, one pointing downward), and choose Add Space Before Paragraph. In my version of Word that adds a 12 point space before the selected paragraphs.

If you want more control over the spacing around your paragraphs, right-click in your document and choose Paragraph to bring up the Paragraph dialogue box. The third section of the Indent and Spacing tab covers Spacing. On the left side you can see options for Before and After with arrows up and down. You can either type in a spacing value or you can use the arrows to choose the value you want.

If you set your paragraphs to have spacing both before and after, the space between two paragraphs will be the higher of those two values not the combination of them. (So if you say 12 point before and 6 point after, the spacing between them will be 12 point not 18 point.)

If you just wanted spacing at the top of a section of paragraphs or at the bottom of a section of paragraphs, you can click the box to say don't add spacing to paragraphs of the same style. Or just add paragraph spacing to that top-most or bottom-most paragraph. Usually this will come into play when you're dealing with a numbered list and want to separate it from the paragraphs of text above and below, but don't want that separation within your list.

If you don't want a space that is there, you can choose Remove Space After Paragraph from the dropdown in the Paragraph section of the Home tab. If you use this method, just be sure you've selected the correct paragraph (the one before the space you want to remove). Or, you can open the Paragraph dialogue box and change the paragraph spacing values for before and after to zero.

(Paragraph spacing is one of those issues that can become a nightmare in a large document where multiple users have been making edits. This is where sometimes using Format Painter to get the spacing between paragraphs consistent can be a lifesaver.)

OTHER FUNCTIONS

We've talked about how to enter text into Word and how to format that text once you've entered it and how to format your paragraphs. But there are a few more basics we need to cover that don't really have anything to do with entering or formatting your text, although they may lead to changes in your text.

Let's start with Find and Replace.

FIND

If you want to find a particular word or phrase in a Word document and you don't want to scan through the whole document, you'll need to use Find. It's very easy.

There are a few ways to do it (as is the case with most of the older functions in Word).

First, you can type Ctrl + F. In earlier versions of Word this would've brought up the Find and Replace dialogue box. In newer versions of Word this may instead just take your cursor to the Navigation search box on the left-hand side of the screen. If all you're looking for is a simple word or phrase, type it into the search box.

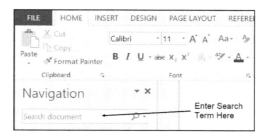

(Depending on how your document is set up, that search box may already be there for you to use. It is in my current document.)

Once you type a word into the search document box, Word will highlight that word or phrase throughout your document and tell you just below the search box how many total results there were. You can either scan through the document for all highlights of your search term or use the arrows next to the number of results to find the matches.

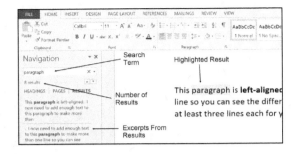

If you click on RESULTS directly under the search box, Word will show you a small snippet of each result on the left-hand side of the screen. In larger documents when you're looking for a very specific usage, scanning the results list can save time. For example, in this document when I just searched for "word" there were 92 matches. It's easier to look at the results list than scan through a thirty page document to look at each highlighted result.

To close your search, just click on the X next to the search term or hit Esc.

Another way to initiate Find is to go to the Editing section of the Home tab (on the far right) and click on Find from there.

But Find is more powerful than this basic search. You can do an Advanced Find that searches by formatting or limits your search results based on various criteria. To do that, you need to bring up the Find and Replace dialogue box.

One way to do so is to go to the Editing Section of the Home tab and click on the small black arrow next to Find. From the dropdown menu select Advanced Find. (Another way to do so is to type Ctrl +H and then click on the Find tab of the Find and Replace dialogue box.)

At first the Find tab doesn't look much more interesting than a basic search. That is until you click on the More option at the bottom left corner, which brings up a number of different search options.

Two of the most important options I use are "Match Case" and "Find Whole Words Only".

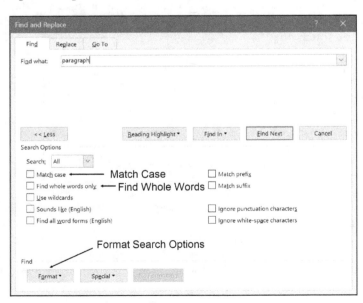

Match Case will look at the search term you enter and only find words with the same capitalization. So if you search for "CAT" and you check this box it will only locate "CAT" for you. If you didn't check this box, it would also locate "cat". (In this case CAT stands for consolidated audit trail and cat is an animal.) When searching for a proper name or an abbreviation like that, I recommend always checking this box.

Find Whole Words Only will only search for the entire word you enter. So again, with the example of "CAT", if you just searched Word normally it would return any word that has "cat" in it. So "category" and "implication" would be returned along with "CAT" and "cat."

Using Match Case and Find Whole Words saves you time when used with Find, but they can be vitally important when used with Replace.

Those are the only two options I use of the ones listed in that section. I can envision how some of the others would be useful, but I've ever needed them in twenty-plus years of using Word. What I have used is the Format option in the bottom left corner. If you click on that it will bring up a dropdown menu of options. One of them is Font.

Clicking on Font will bring up a Find Font dialogue box where you can specify the formatting you want to search for. In the screenshot below, I've chosen to find all text in italics. You can see it selected in the Find Font dialogue box and after I clicked on OK it was added under my search term.

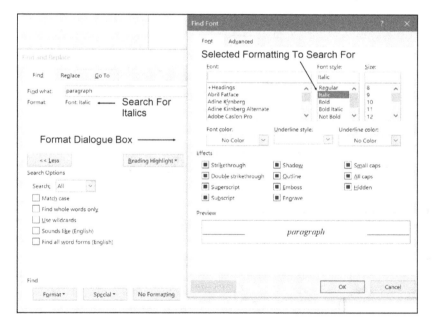

To find all italic text in the document, leave the search term box blank. When you click on search Word will show you all of the italic text in your document. This works for any type of formatting you want to find in your document and is good for combinations of formatting.

If all you want is to find text in italics (or text that's bolded or underlined), another way to do this is to click into the search box and then use the control key shortcuts. Typing Ctrl + I once will change the search so that you're looking for italicized text. Typing it another time will change the search so that you're looking for text that isn't in italics. Typing it a third time will remove it from the search.

Be careful when using the formatting search options that you don't forget to change an option and end up missing a search result you wanted to see. (For example, leaving it with no italics when you want all instances of a certain word, even those in italics.)

One last point. If you click on Special at the bottom of the Find and Replace dialogue box you'll see a list of special characters or attributes that you can also search on such as tabs and em dashes.

REPLACE

Find is useful. Replace is fantastic.

I have a bad habit with my novels of deciding after the novel is written that a character name needs to be changed. For example, I had a 90,000-word novel with a medic whose name was Marian. After reading Medic Marian one too many times I decided she needed a new name. But manually changing it would've been a nightmare. Find and Replace took care of it in less than a minute.

Same with fixing two spaces after a period. That's how I was taught to do things in school, so it's instinct by now. But there's a lot of negativity towards using two spaces after a period in the writing community, so now when I finish writing a piece I use find and replace to replace all instances of two spaces with one. I get to type the way I'm used to and I also get to deprive those judgey judgey types an opportunity to be nasty. Win win.

Having said that…

It's easy to mess up find and replace. Usually by not thinking through the implications of the changes you're going to make. Like in the example we had above with CAT. Let's say your boss wants you to replace all uses of CAT with consolidated audit trail. So you do. You do a quick find and replace for CAT and think you're done. Problem is, if you didn't think this through and use Find Whole Words Only and Match Case you also just replaced the "cat" in implication with "consolidated audit trail." Now you have a place somewhere in your document that reads "impliconsolidated audit trailion." Hopefully you'd catch that in spellcheck. But you wouldn't catch an instance where you replaced "cat", meaning the animal, with consolidated audit trail. You'd have some very confused readers when they reached the point where the firemen rescued the consolidated audit trail from the tree.

(I know. That's ridiculous and would never happen. But other things like that have happened.) Not what you want.

So the basics. To find text (or formatting) in your document and replace it, you can use Ctrl + H to bring up the Find and Replace dialogue box or you can go to the Editing section of the Home tab and click on Replace.

What you'll see is a Find What box and a Replace With box. In the Find What box type what you want to find. In the Replace With box type what you want to replace it with. So when I'm hunting down double spaces after a period I click into the Find What box and type two spaces and then click into the Replace With box and type a single space. Next, I click on Replace All and Word replaces all of the two spaces in the document and tells me how many replacements it made.

If you want to be more careful about what you're replacing, you can instead click on Replace. Word will locate the next instance of what you told it to find and highlight it. Click Replace again to replace the text that's highlighted with what you told it to use for the replacement. Word will do so and then go on to the next instance. If you don't want to replace that one, click on Find Next until you do find an instance you want to replace. When you do, click on Replace.

As with Find, you have the More option that lets you find whole words, match the case of your search term, and search by formatting.

Here's an example of a find/replace where I'm looking for instances of "paragraph" that aren't in italics and replacing them with "paragraph" in italics.

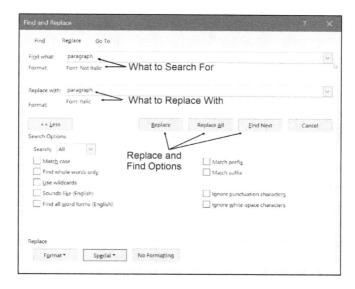

One other item to note. When Word does the find and replace, it will sometimes do so only from where you are in the document forward. When this happens it tells you how many items it found and replaced and then asks if you want to continue searching from the beginning. To be sure that you've found all instances, say yes.

SPELLING AND GRAMMAR CHECK

Unless you've done something to your settings or are working in a document that's already hundreds of pages long, you'll notice little red and blue squiggly lines appear under some words as you type. This is Word's real-time spelling and grammar check at work.

> As with Find, you can also fine-tune your search by clicking on More. This is where Match Case and Find Whole Words Only are incredibly powerful. No accidentally replacing all instances of "tom" with "bill" including changing "tomorrow" into "billorrow".

In the image above, there's a red squiggly line under "billorow" because that's not a real word, so Word identified it as a misspelling. The blue squiggly line under "More" is there because Word thinks that's a potential grammar error since I have a word capitalized in the middle of a sentence.

For spelling errors, you can right-click on the word and Word will suggest possible spellings if you're close enough to the actual spelling for it to guess the word. For grammar errors, it'll suggest the fix as well, but I usually leave those until the end when I run Spelling and Grammar check on the entire document.

The Spelling & Grammar check can be found in the Review tab on the left side in the Proofing section.

Spelling and Grammar Check

Once you click on it, Word will walk its way through your entire document checking for spelling and grammar issues. When it finds one it will display on the right side of the screen the issue it found and what it suggests as possible ways to fix it. You can ignore the suggestion, agree to the suggestion (by clicking on Change), or click into the document and type in your own edit to fix the issue.

With spelling errors, you can also choose to Ignore All if this is a word that's used repeatedly throughout the document but is not an error. (Like a made-up name or industry abbreviation.) In the alternative, you can choose to Change All if you think this is an error you've made more than once and you trust that there's never a time the word was used that doesn't need changed.

As you can see below, with spelling errors sometimes Word gives you multiple alternative words to choose from. Be sure you click on the correct one before selecting Change.

A word of caution when using the spelling and grammar check: Word is very good with spelling errors. It's not so good with grammar issues. More than once it has suggested the wrong version of its and it's to me. And it often fails to parse complex sentences properly, so ends up suggesting me instead of I when it shouldn't. You can read the explanations it gives, but don't assume that just because Word flagged a potential grammar error that it's right. Do not use it blindly. You will introduce errors into your document if you do.

When Word finishes with the spelling and grammar check it will display a Readability Statistics dialogue box. I sometimes find it interesting to know what grade level I've written to, but it's mostly useless for day-to-day purposes. Just close it out.

Also, once you've run spellcheck on a document and told Word to ignore spelling or grammar errors, it will continue to do so in that document. To run a clean spelling and grammar check of your document, go to the File tab and click on Options. Next, click on Proofing and click on the gray box labeled Recheck Document. This will show you a notice that you're about to reset the spelling and grammar check. Click OK. Now when you look at the document all spelling and grammar errors will be shown once more and when you run the spelling and grammar check it will show you everything it considers a spelling or grammar error.

WORD COUNT

One piece of information that can be useful in that Readability Statistics dialogue box is the word count of your document. Some short story markets, for example, have word count limits and some online forms restrict you to a certain number of characters. To see how many characters or words are in your document (or in a selection from your document), go to the Proofing section of the Review tab and choose Word Count. You'll now see the Word Count dialogue box which tells you the number of words, number of characters, and number of characters without spaces for your document or selection.

Your current word count is also usually visible in the bottom left corner of your document.

PAGE FORMATTING

We talked about how to format individual text and how to format paragraphs, but we still need to cover how to format a page. This is more relevant for when you want to print a document, which is why I saved it until this point.

PAGE NUMBERING

If you're going to print your document, you'll likely want to number the pages in the document. DO NOT do this manually. Word will do this for you and by letting Word do this, you ensure that the page numbering isn't changed when you make edits to the document.

To add page numbers to your document, go to the Header & Footer section of the Insert tab and click on the arrow next to Page Number. This will bring up a dropdown menu that lets you choose where on the page you want your page numbers to display and then how you want those page numbers to look.

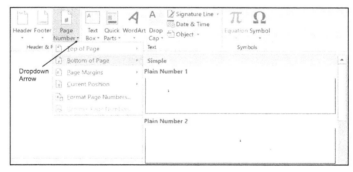

That should be all you need. Go there, choose Bottom of Page, Plain Number 2, and you'll have a document that has a page number centered at the bottom of each page.

In *Intermediate Word* I talk about how to create section breaks so that you have different page numbering in different parts of your document, but for basic, simple, page numbering you don't need to do more than I just showed you.

HEADERS AND FOOTERS

If you want text to repeat at the top or bottom of every page, then you should use headers and footers. Again, don't try to manually put this information into your document. One little change to your text and it'll break. (Not to mention how it'll look on an ereader.)

A header goes at the top of your page.

A footer goes at the bottom of your page.

To add one, go to the Header & Footer section of the Insert tab and click on the arrow below the one you need (header or footer), and then choose the option that works best for you, just like you did with page numbering.

You're not stuck with the format you choose. For example, with short story submissions, they usually want the header to be in the top right corner. If you choose the Blank header option, that creates a header that's in the top left corner. But you can simply go to the Home tab and choose to right-align the text in your header and that will put it in the right corner instead.

After you choose your header or footer option, Word inserts [Type here] into the designated spots where you're supposed to put text. To edit this text, just start typing because it will already be highlighted in gray. If it isn't, select the text and then start typing. Text in your header or footer works just like text in your document. You can use the same options from the Home tab to change your font, font size, color, etc.

Headers and footers are in a separate area from the main text of your document. So if you're in a header or footer and want to go back to the main document, you can (1) click on Close Header and Footer in the menu bar, (2) hit the Esc key on your keyboard, or (3) double-click on the main text in your document which will be grayed out while you're in the header or footer.

If you're in your main document and want to open a header or footer, you can (1) double-click on the text in the header or footer, or (2) right-click on the header or footer and choose "Edit Header" or "Edit Footer" from the dropdown options. I've found in recent versions of Word that double-clicking when there's just a page number in the footer doesn't work well for me and that I have to right-click and choose Edit Footer instead. This was not true of older versions of Word.

MARGINS

Margins are the white space along the edges of your document. The default in my version of Word is one-inch margins all around which is what most submission guidelines I've seen require, so you usually won't need to edit these. But in case you do...

(Because it looks like at least in Word 2003 the margins were not one inch all around.)

Go to the Page Layout tab and under the Page Setup section click on the dropdown under Margins. You will see some standard choices to choose from or the option at the bottom to set custom margins. If you click on Custom Margins, it will take you to the Page Setup dialogue box where you can specify the margins for top, bottom, left, and right.

You can also open the Page Setup dialogue box directly by clicking on the expansion arrow for the Page Setup section.

PAGE ORIENTATION

A standard document has a page orientation of portrait. That's where the long edge of the document is along the sides and the short edge is across the bottom and top. This is how most books, business reports, and school papers are formatted, and it's the default in Word.

But sometimes you'll create a document where you need to turn the text ninety degrees so that the long edge is at the top and bottom and the short edge is on the sides. A lot of tables in appendixes are done this way. And presentation slides are often this way. That's called landscape orientation.

(Think paintings here. A drawing of a person—a portrait—is taller than it is wide. A drawing of a mountain range—a landscape—is wider than it is tall.)

To change the orientation of your document, go to the Page Setup section of the Page Layout tab, click on the arrow under Orientation, and choose the orientation you want.

(If you use section breaks--which are covered in *Intermediate Word*—you can set the page orientation on a section-by-section basis. But if you're not using sections changing the orientation on any page will change the orientation of the entire document.)

PRINTING

Printing in Word, at its most basic, is incredibly easy. You can simply type Ctrl + P or go to File and choose Print from the list of options on the left-hand side. Both options will bring you to the Print screen.

On the right-hand side you can see what the document will look like when it prints. For documents that are longer than a page, you can use the arrows at the bottom to navigate through the document preview. If everything looks good, you can just click on the Print icon.

But there are some changes you can make at this stage, so let's walk through them.

COPIES

Right next to the Print icon you can specify the number of copies of the document you want to print. The default is one copy. To increase that amount, either type a new number into the box or use the arrows on the right-hand side.

PRINTER

Your default printer should already be showing under the printer option. Sometimes I will change this to print to Microsoft XPS Document Writer or, if I'm working on a corporate computer, a PDF. This is for when I don't want to print a physical copy of the document but would like to have a version that can't be easily edited. (You can also use Save As to create a PDF version.)

SETTINGS: PRINT ALL PAGES OR PAGES

Below the printer choice are all the Settings options. In the Print All Pages and Pages section just below it you can choose to print just a subset of the pages in your document. For example, sometimes I just want to print one section or one page of a document.

You can choose from the dropdown to print the current page, print text that you've selected (print selection), only print odd pages, or only print even pages.

In the Pages box you can list individual page numbers that you want to print. For page ranges, use a dash. For a list of individual pages, use commas. So if you want to print pages 3, 5, and 7 you would enter "3,5,7" in the Pages box. If you wanted to print pages 3 *through* 7, you would enter "3-7" in the box. When you enter a page range in the Pages box it changes the dropdown menu to "Custom Print."

SETTINGS: PRINT ONE-SIDED OR TWO-SIDED

The default is for Word to print on one side of the page, but you can change it to print two-sided documents. To do so, click on the arrow next to the default choice of one-sided. You'll now see a dropdown with four options, one-sided, both sides with the long edge, both sides with the short edge, and manually print on both sides.

Choose the manual option if you have a printer that isn't set up to print two-sided documents.

Choose to flip pages on the long edge for documents with a portrait orientation. (This will be most documents.) Choose to flip pages on the short edge for documents with a landscape orientation.

SETTINGS: COLLATION

This is only relevant if you're printing more than one copy of a document that's more than one page long.

The default when printing multiple copies of a document is to print one entire copy of the document and then print the next copy of the document. (That's the collated option that shows 1,2,3 and then 1,2,3.)

The other option you can choose is to print all of your page ones and then all of your page twos and then all of your page threes. (That's the uncollated option that shows 1,1,1 and 2,2,2, etc.) The uncollated option is useful for situations where you might be giving out handouts one page at a time, but generally you'll want to stick with collated copies.

SETTINGS: ORIENTATION

We talked about this one before, but if you want the text on your page to go across the long edge instead of the short edge, this is another place where you can make that selection. The default is Portrait Orientation, but if you click on the arrow, you can instead choose Landscape Orientation.

SETTINGS: PAPER SIZE

The default in Word (at least in the U.S. version) is to print on 8.5"x11" paper. If you want to print your document on a different size of paper (say A4 or legal), then this is where you'd change that setting.

There are an insane number of choices both on the dropdown menu and if you click on More Paper Sizes but for most documents you'll probably be using the default.

If you do change the paper size, make sure that your printer has the correct paper in it.

SETTINGS: MARGINS

We already talked about how to change the margins on your document, but this is another place where you can do that. You have a list of pre-formatted options as well as the ability to customize.

SETTINGS: PAGES TO PRINT PER SHEET

If you want to save paper because perhaps you're reviewing a document and it's not the final version, you can print more than one page of your document onto a single sheet.

The default is to print one page on one sheet, but if you click on the dropdown menu here you can choose to print 2, 4, 6, 8, or 16 pages per sheet. You can also choose to scale your text to a chosen paper size.

Be careful with this, because Word will let you make a choice that results in an illegible document. Four pages on one is still legible, but I suspect that sixteen pages on one page would be virtually useless. (Unless you're in a situation where your teacher said you could bring one page of notes and you're trying to cram an entire semester's worth of knowledge on that one page.)

PAGE SETUP

As a beginner, I'd ignore the Page Setup link at the bottom of the page. Most of what it covers we've already addressed above. It's just the older way of specifying your print settings.

CUSTOMIZED SETTINGS

We're almost done, but before we wrap up I want to talk about how to customize your version of Word. I've already mentioned the Quick Access Toolbar, but there are some other settings I routinely adjust in order to get Word to work for me in the way I want it to.

Everything we're going to talk about in this section can be found in the File tab under Options with the exception of the last one which is found in the File tab under Info.

So first go to the File tab and from there click on Options. This will bring up the Word Options dialogue box (below).

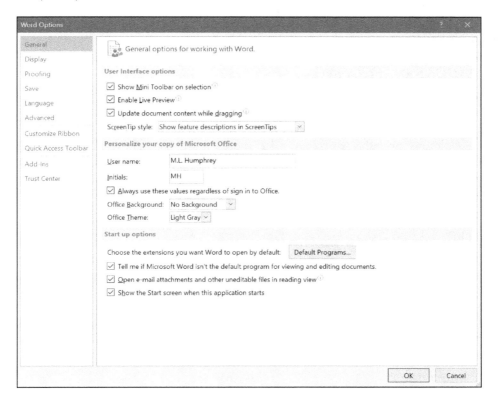

If there's a setting in Word that's giving you problems, chances are the way to fix it is buried somewhere in this dialogue box. I'll walk you through a few key things I change, but you might find it worthwhile to explore on your own. Just be warned that any changes you make here will affect *all* of your Word documents, not just this one. So be careful.

(And if you're using someone else's version of Word and wondering why it looks so different, changes they've made here could very well be the reason.)

FILE -> OPTIONS -> GENERAL SETTINGS

This is where you can customize how your user name and initials will display for things like track changes, adding comments, and document properties. (None of which we've discussed so far but which you may run into if you're working on group documents.)

If you're going to change this, like I have, you also need to check the box that says to always use these values. If you don't, newer versions of Word that use your Windows login will override what you put here.

FILE -> OPTIONS -> DISPLAY

I'm pretty sure I've customized this one by clicking on the box that says to show white space between pages in print layout view. Without this box checked, you can't visually see page breaks in your document. One page of text rolls right into the next with just a thin gray line to indicate a page break. It's fine when you're dealing with longer pages of text or a report without breaks, but when you have very short chapters or sections, you can end up with three or four of them displayed on a single page. That annoys me, so I change it.

FILE -> OPTIONS -> PROOFING

This one I always have to mess with.

My former day job involves a lot of rule citations, where you write things like Rule 3070(c). Unfortunately for me, one of the proofing defaults in Word is to automatically convert (c) into the copyright sign. That's probably very handy for most of the population, but a complete pain for someone like me. So every time I get a new version of Word, I have to remove that one from the list of AutoCorrect Options.

In the other tabs in this section you'll find things like replacing straight quotes with smart quotes (which you're supposed to do for fiction writing). To get this one to actually change, you have to make that change in two tabs, the AutoFormat as You Type tab and the AutoFormat tab.

This is also the area of Word where I have a setting that converts typing two dashes in a row into an em-dash. (If you do this, you need to space after the next word to get the conversion to happen. And if the word is a contraction you actually need to space before the apostrophe to get it to convert. So dash, dash, word, space and you'll get –word but type dash, dash, word and you'll just have --word.)

A lot of the autocorrect options are very handy—I often type too fast and mistype "the" and Word always catches that for me—but do keep an eye out for "errors" you don't want fixed as you type.

It's probably a good idea to take a look through the tabs just to make sure there aren't any listed that you know you won't want to use.

This is also the section where you can create a Custom Dictionary if your company allows it. For example, my first name is always flagged by spellcheck. When I can, I add it to my custom dictionary so I don't get a spelling alert every time I send an email.

This is also where you can customize the settings for the spelling and grammar check. I usually use the default settings, but if you don't want to have Word flagging issues as you type, this is where you can turn that off.

FILE -> OPTIONS -> SAVE

In this section can specify how often Word saves a recovery version of your document. This can be a life saver if your computer or Word crash while you're working.

I always have autorecovery turned on even though it can be annoying. For some reason the CreateSpace templates take forever to save the autorecovery version. And the document freezes while it's doing it. But all it takes is losing something you were working on once to appreciate how important autorecovery can be.

You can specify here how often Word should save and where it should store that file. In newer versions of Word when Word crashes the next time it opens you'll be given the option of opening the recovered version and/or the last saved version.

If that doesn't happen, notice here where those files are saved. There's a chance that you may be able to go to that location and recover the file you need from there.

Best practice, though, is to make a habit of saving your files on a regular basis even if you're not done with them yet.

FILE -> OPTIONS -> ADVANCED

There are a ton of options in this section. I don't recall changing any of these in my own personal version of Word, but you might want to glance through to see if there's something you want to change. (And it's possible that I did change one of these a couple years ago and now just don't remember it. I'm used to Word working in a certain way and when it doesn't I usually go looking for a way to fix it or change it to what I'm familiar with. But with all the choices in File -> Options, you only need to change them once and then they're that way for that version of Word forever or until you change them back.)

FILE -> OPTIONS -> CUSTOMIZE RIBBON

If you want to get really fancy, you can customize the content of the tabs at the top of the screen. Say you want everything you think you'll use consolidated onto your Home tab or know you'll never need to use Styles and want to remove them, you can do it. However…

I would advise against this. Because your customization will only exist in your current version of Word. It won't exist on your IT guy's version. It won't exist on your best friend's. It won't exist on the version that everyone else is using when they answer questions on the internet. Which means once you do this, you're on your own. Other people won't be able to tell you where to go in your version of Word to make something happen.

And, the minute you upgrade to a new version of Word or start a new job, you'll be back to using the standard layout.

FILE -> OPTIONS -> QUICK ACCESS TOOLBAR

This is another location for you to customize what appears on the Quick Access Toolbar, and this one I do customize. I've added Select All, Breaks, and Format Painter here.

FILE -> INFO

If you go to the File tab and click on Info, there are a few more things you can do with respect to your document that you need to know about. I hesitate to tell you about this, because people using it have caused me more issues than I can tell you. But since it may come up and is useful to know about, I'm going to tell you. Just be careful with this one, please. I can't help you if you screw this up.

Okay.

So when you work on a file in Word it stores a bunch of information behind the scenes including who the author of the document was. Sometimes, when you're going to share a document with a client or someone outside of your group, you'll want to strip that information out of your document and anonymize it to the extent you can. And if you've used comments or track changes in your document, it's a very good idea to make sure those are all removed before you pass the document outside of your team. (No one needs to see that back and forth you had over that paragraph on page five.)

The way you review your document for information you might want to remove is by going to the Info section of the File tab and clicking on Check for Issues next to Inspect Document, and then choosing to Inspect Document. This will scan your document for all sorts of things like comments, personal information, embedded documents, collapsed headings, etc.

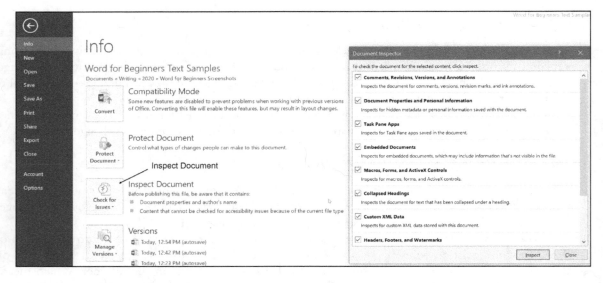

Some of this is very useful to check for. Some not so much. Like headers, footers, and watermarks. Chances are you wanted those in your document, so after you scan your document and Word offers to remove all of them, BE VERY CAREFUL. You can destroy a lot of work with just a click or two.

What I recommend if you're going to do this is that you save a copy of the file beforehand and then save the inspected and stripped down version as a new file. That way if you delete something you shouldn't, you can go back and fix it.

And always wait until the absolute end to strip out the personalization. I've been in situations where someone did this mid-review of a document and then everyone's comments on that document (and there were four or five of us providing comments) were listed as by Author. Believe it or not, that's a big deal. Because it matters whether that comment to edit something on page three was made by your boss or the new intern who doesn't know what they're doing but thinks they do.

So be careful. This one is useful but potentially dangerous.

CONCLUSION

Alright. There you have it. Enough knowledge about Word to let you do most of what you need to do. In *Intermediate Word* I dive into how to create complex numbered lists, insert tables, use section breaks, insert a table of contents, use styles, add watermarks and hyperlinks, deal with track changes, and more. Things that you may need to do at some point, but aren't essential.

If you found this guide easy to follow and want to learn that, then *Intermediate Word* is available for purchase. But there are other options. Now that you know the basics of Word, if you run into something you want to do but don't know how to do it, you can research how to do it either through Word or online.

First, within Word.

Hover your mouse over any of the options at the top of the screen and you'll see a basic description of what it does. For many of those options, at the bottom of the description is a question mark with the words Tell Me More. If you click on those words, you'll be taken to Word's built-in help function.

You can also click on the question mark in the top right corner of Word to bring up Word's built-in help function and then search for what you need to know.

I'll tell you, though. Nine times out of ten I search the help function in Word and give up after about a minute because what it says is nowhere close to what I need to know. But I always start there, just in case.

Usually, I end up doing an internet search for what I'm looking for using "microsoft word" as part of my search string. So I might search for "how to add a hyperlink microsoft word."

I then click on the result with the web address support.microsoft.com.

Bizarre as it is, given the general worthlessness of the built-in help function, the help provided on the Microsoft website is actually very good. If you want to know how something works, the website will almost always provide the information you need.

But it doesn't work so well with the "can I do X" sort of questions. (This is more often a problem with Excel than Word because there's only so much you can do in Word and it's mostly functional.)

If I have a "can I do X" sort of question, I do the exact same internet search as above, but instead of expecting an answer from Microsoft, I read through the top handful of results to see if anyone has asked my question before on a public forum and had it answered. Usually someone has.

If you still can't figure it out at that point (or even before that), you can also email me at mlhumphreywriter@gmail.com. I'm happy to point you in the right direction or figure out the answer myself. I don't check that email address every day, so you may have to wait a few days for me to get back to you, but I will get back to you eventually.

If all else fails, there are forums both on the Microsoft website and elsewhere where you can ask your question. Just be prepared for someone to imply that you're foolish or stupid for asking. I don't know why those types of forums are so obnoxious, but they are. It takes a bit of a thick skin to wade through and get the answer you need. Also, if you go that route, don't click on links from strangers. And be wary of anything that has you messing around in restricted files on your computer. It might work, it might break your computer.

Okay. So that's it. You should know the basics of Word at this point, and you now have the tools to find more answers if you need them. Good luck with it!

Intermediate Word

WORD ESSENTIALS BOOK 2

M.L. HUMPHREY

CONTENTS

INTRODUCTION

In *Word for Beginners* we walked through the basics of what you need to know in order to use Word on a day-to-day basis, including how to open a file, how to enter text, how to format that text as well as your paragraphs and your document overall, customizing Word to meet your needs, and printing and saving your document.

But there's a lot more you can do in Word.

If you use Word in a business setting, chances are you'll also want to know how to create and format a table, insert images into your document, have Word create a table of contents for you, use Styles, track changes, insert comments, and use section and page breaks to allow for different page formatting in the same document. We're going to cover all of that as well as some fairly simple things you can do in Word, like add hyperlinks, watermarks, and numbered lines to your document.

There are some aspects of Word I'm still not going to cover in this guide, mostly design-based functions like creating SmartArt or using WordArt. By the time you're done with this guide you should be comfortable enough in Word to explore those on your own if you want to, but I don't consider them core uses of Word that most people need to know, whereas I've used track changes in every corporate job I've had.

Also, this guide is written using Word 2013. If you're using an earlier version of Word, there may be things I do that you can't, although I don't think that will happen often. Word may look different to you if you're in a really old version of Word, but I'll try to cover multiple ways to do that same thing so that hopefully at least one option will work for you. For those in Word 2016 you may have some functionality I don't (like real-time editing by more than one user), but that doesn't mean that's what's covered here won't be of value to you.

And I'm working in Compatibility Mode. What that means is that there may be some fancier aspects to Word that I can't use, but I'm a big believer in creating documents that are as accessible as possible. If you agree with that approach, it's a good habit to get into to work in Compatibility Mode. (I learned this lesson the hard way when I used a function in Excel that a client didn't have in their version of Excel and had to redo an entire week's worth of work so they could use the spreadsheet I'd created for them.) Anyway.

Let's get started by reviewing some basic terminology.

BASIC TERMINOLOGY

Below are some basic terms that I'll use throughout this guide. I want to make sure that you're familiar with them before we start.

TAB

I refer to the menu choices at the top of the screen (File, Home, Insert, Design, Page Layout, References, Mailings, Review, View, Developer) as tabs. If you click on one you'll see that the way it's highlighted sort of looks like an old-time filing system.

Each tab you select will show you different options. For example, in the image above, I have the Home tab selected and you can do various tasks such as cut/copy/paste, format paint, change the font, change the formatting of a paragraph, apply a style to your text, find/replace words in your document, or select the text in your document. Other tabs give other options.

CLICK

If I tell you to click on something, that means to use your mouse (or trackpad) to move the arrow on the screen over to a specific location and left-click or right-click on the option. (See the next definition for the difference between left-click and right-click).

If you left-click, this selects the item. If you right-click, this generally creates a dropdown list of options to choose from. If I don't tell you which to do, left- or right-click, then left-click.

LEFT-CLICK/RIGHT-CLICK

If you look at your mouse or your trackpad, you generally have two flat buttons to press. One is on the left side, one is on the right. If I say left-click that means to press down on the button on the left. If I say right-click that means press down on the button on the right.

Now, as I sadly learned when I had to upgrade computers and ended up with an HP Envy, not all track pads have the left- and right-hand buttons. In that case, you'll basically want to press on either the bottom left-hand side of the track pad or the bottom right-hand side of the trackpad. Since you're working blind it may take a little trial and error to get the option you want working. (Or is that just me?)

SELECT OR HIGHLIGHT

If I tell you to select text, that means to left-click at the end of the text you want to select, hold that left-click, and move your cursor to the other end of the text you want to select.

Another option is to use the Shift key. Go to one end of the text you want to select. Hold down the shift key and use the arrow keys to move to the other end of the text you want to select. If you arrow up or down, that will select an entire row at a time.

With both methods, which side of the text you start on doesn't matter. You can start at the end and go to the beginning or start at the beginning and go to the end. Just start at one end or the other of the text you want to select.

The text you've selected will then be highlighted in gray.

If you need to select text that isn't touching you can do this by selecting your first section of text and then holding down the Ctrl key and selecting your second section of text using your mouse. (You can't arrow to the second section of text or you'll lose your already selected text.)

DROPDOWN MENU

If you right-click in a Word document, you will see what I'm going to refer to as a dropdown menu. (Sometimes it will actually drop upward if you're towards the bottom of the document.)

A dropdown menu provides you a list of choices to select from.

There are also dropdown menus available for some of the options listed under the tabs at the top of the screen. For example, if you go to the Home tab, you'll see small arrows below or next to some of the options, like the numbered list option in the paragraph section. If you click on those arrows, you'll see that there are multiple choices you can choose from listed on a dropdown menu.

EXPANSION ARROWS

I don't know the official word for these, but you'll also notice at the bottom right corner of most of the sections in each tab that there are little arrows. If you hold your mouse over the arrow it lets you bring up a more detailed set of options, usually through a dialogue box (which we'll discuss next).

In the Home tab, for example, there are expansion arrows for Clipboard, Font, Paragraph, and Styles. Holding your mouse over the arrow will give a brief description of what clicking on the expansion arrow will do.

DIALOGUE BOX

Dialogue boxes are pop-up boxes that cover specialized settings. As just mentioned, if you click on an expansion arrow, it will often open a dialogue box that contains more choices than are visible in that section. When you right-click in a Word document and choose Font, Paragraph, or Hyperlink that also opens dialogue boxes.

Dialogue boxes allow the most granular level of control over an option. For example, the Paragraph Dialogue Box has more options available than in the Paragraph section of the Home tab.

(This may not apply to you, but be aware that if you have more than one Word document open and open a dialogue box in one of those documents, you may not be able to move to the other documents you have open until you close the dialogue box.)

SCROLL BAR

This is more useful in Excel than in Word, but on the right-hand side of the screen you should see a scroll bar. You can either click in the space above or below the bar to move up or down a small amount or you can left-click on the bar, hold the left-click, and drag the bar up or down to move through the document more quickly. You can also use the arrows at the top and the bottom of the bar to move up and down through your document. (The scroll bar isn't always visible in Word. If you don't see it, move your mouse over to the side of the screen and it should appear.)

In general, you shouldn't see a scroll bar at the bottom of the screen, but it is possible. This would happen if you ever change the zoom level of your document to the point that you're not seeing the entire width of the document in a single screen. (Not something I recommend when working with normal documents.)

ARROW

If I ever tell you to arrow to the left or right or up or down, that just means use your arrow keys. This will move your cursor to the left one space, to the right one space, up one line, or down one line. If you're at the end of a line and arrow to the right, it will take you to the beginning of the next line. If you're at the beginning of a line and arrow to the left, it will take you to the end of the last line.

CURSOR

There are two possible meanings for cursor. One is the one I just used. In your Word document, you will see that there is a blinking line. This indicates where you are in the document. If you type text, each letter will appear where the cursor was at the time you typed it. The cursor will move (at least in the U.S. and I'd assume most European versions) to the right as you type. This version of the cursor should be visible at all times unless you have text selected.

The other type of cursor is the one that's tied to the movement of your mouse or trackpad. When you're typing, it will not be visible. But stop typing and move your mouse or trackpad, and you'll see it. If the cursor is positioned over your text, it will look somewhat like a tall skinny capital I. If you move it up to the menu options or off to the sides, it becomes a white arrow. (Except for when you position it over any option under the tabs that can be typed in such as Font Size or Font when it once again looks like a skinny capital I.)

Usually I won't refer to your cursor, I'll just say, "click" or "select" or whatever action you need to take with it, but moving the cursor to that location will be implied.

QUICK ACCESS TOOLBAR

You might notice that the options in the very top left corner of my version of Word are different from what you see. That's because I've customized the Quick Access Toolbar. You can do this on your version of Word by clicking on the arrow you see at the very end of the list and then checking the commands you want to have available there. It can be useful if there's something you're doing repeatedly (like inserting section breaks) that's located on a different tab than something else you're doing repeatedly (like formatting text).

Of course, it's only useful if you use it. Half the time I forget I've done that. But if you can remember, it's a nice time-saver.

CONTROL SHORTCUTS

I'll occasionally mention control shortcuts that you can use to perform tasks. Most of the main ones like save, copy, cut, and paste were already covered in *Word for Beginners*. When I reference them I'll do so by writing it as Ctrl + a capital letter. To use the shortcut just hold down the control key while typing the letter specified. Even though the letter will be capitalized, you don't need to use the capitalized version for the shortcut to work. For example, holding down the Ctrl key and the s key at the same time will save your document. I'll write this as Ctrl + S.

A FEW SIMPLE TRICKS

This chapter covers a few tricks in Word that you might want to know that aren't going to come up all the time. It's a bit of a mish-mash, so let's just dive right in.

HYPERLINKS

If you want to add a link from your document to an outside source, whether that's a file or a website, you can do so with a hyperlink.

The simplest and probably most common type of hyperlink is to a website. One way to add one is to just copy the website address or type it into your document: www.yahoo.com.

Word will automatically treat a properly formatted website address as a hyperlink. (This is in newer versions of Word. If you have a really old version of Word I don't think it used to do that.) For a website address to be properly formatted it needs the www portion of the address included.

If you enter a website address and don't want it to be hyperlinked, when Word converts it to a hyperlink (you'll know because it'll turn the text blue and underline it), just use Ctrl + Z to undo the hyperlinking. You'll be left with the website address, but the link will be gone.

Of course, a lot of website addresses are long and ugly and you may not want to include the full address in your document. In that case, you can use any text in your document to link to the website address. For example, I might write "You can access that website here" with a hyperlink tied to the word "here".

To do that, select the word or words you want to turn into a hyperlink and go to the Links section of the Insert tab and click on Hyperlink. This will bring up the Insert Hyperlink dialogue box. Your cursor will be shown in the Address box at the bottom of the box. Paste the website address you want into that location and then click OK. You can also click on the dropdown box to see a list of recent websites to choose from and then click on OK after you've selected the one you want.

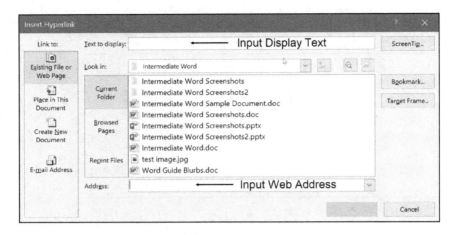

An alternative way to insert a hyperlink is to select the text you want to turn into a hyperlink, right-click, and choose Hyperlink from the dropdown menu.

You can also select your text and then use Ctrl + K to bring up the Insert Hyperlink dialogue box. (I don't insert hyperlinks often enough to have memorized that one.)

* * *

You can link to sources other than websites. In the list of options on the left-hand side of the Insert Hyperlink dialogue box there are also options to use an existing file, a place in the current document, a new document, or an email address.

To link to an existing file, choose that option and then navigate to the file you want using the dropdown menu next to Look In in the Insert Hyperlink dialogue box. It works just like if you were opening a file.

I rarely link to other files, though, because I've worked with documents that did this and the links were often broken. One reason this happens is when someone links to a document that's only available on their computer. It works fine for them, but not for anyone else. Another reason this happens is the linked document is moved or renamed after the link is created.

So be careful with this one. It seems like a great idea, but it rarely is.

You can also use hyperlinks to link to another section of your document. This one I've used often. (And it's how Word's table of contents works, too.)

To do this, you either need to be using headers (e.g., Heading 1 Style) or you need to create a bookmark that you can link to. Creating a bookmark is pretty much the same process as creating a hyperlink. Select the text you want to bookmark, go to the Link section of the Insert tab, and click on Bookmark.

This will bring up the Bookmark dialogue box.

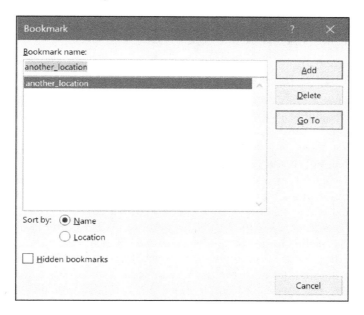

You need to type a name for your bookmark that will make sense to you when it's in a list. It also has to be one word. As soon as you use a space in the name, the option to add the bookmark will disappear. (In the example above I used an underscore to get around that issue and called it another_location.) Once you've created and named your bookmark, you can then add your hyperlink to take the user from the location of the hyperlink to the location of the bookmark.

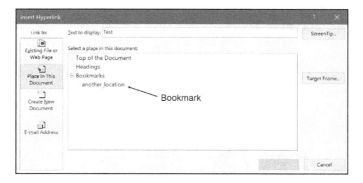

To add an email address you just choose the email address option on the left-hand side and add the email address into the field provided. On this one, I'd recommend also including the email address in the document. When a user clicks on a hyperlink to an email it opens the user's default email program on their computer. In many cases this will not be the email program the user wants to use to email you. For example, I have Gmail accounts I use, but email links always open Outlook on my computer.

What's annoying to me is that I sometimes have to click on those links and let my computer open Outlook just so I can see the email address and then copy it into the email account I actually want to use. So don't do that to your potential audience if you can avoid it. (Even if you have to write the email address as write me [at] gmail.com to get around web scrapers.)

CHANGE CASE

So that was hyperlinks. Let's cover something very simple next: how to change the case of text. You're not likely to need this often, but it is a handy little trick when you do need it.

Say you have a bunch of text that's in all caps (LIKE THIS) and you want to convert it to title case (Like This). Or that's in lower case (like this) and you want to convert it to all caps (LIKE THIS).

You could retype it, but that's annoying and could introduce errors.

If you just need all caps, you could format the text as all caps or small caps using the Font dialogue box. But your options there are limited. (And I believe in older versions of Word that if you copied and pasted that text as text only you'd lose that formatting).

The best way to handle this is to use the Change Case option in the Home tab. Select your text, go to the Font section of the Home tab, and click on the Change Case option. It's in the top row and looks like Aa with a dropdown on the right side. This will give you the option to format your text as sentence case (where the first letter of each new sentence is capitalized), lower case (where no letters are capitalized), upper case (where all letters are capitalized), or capitalize each word (where, you guessed it, each word is capitalized).

There's also toggle case which it appears reverses the capitalization of every letter.

Once you apply the change case option to a section of text it will be permanently changed, which distinguishes this option from using the formatting options in the Font dialogue box.

INSERT OR REMOVE A WATERMARK

Another simple but useful one.

Have you ever seen a document that had DRAFT in gray text across the background? That was what's called a watermark. It can be very handy to use when you circulate a document for review but you want to make it clear that the document should not be considered a final version.

I've seen people put DRAFT in their header or footer instead, but that's just not as effective. Using a watermark is handy because it's visible behind the text so no one can copy the document and conveniently leave off the header or footer. Also, most people know how to edit a header or footer, but a lot of people don't know how to remove a watermark, so it's more likely to stay in place until you're ready to remove it.

To add a watermark to your document, go to the Page Background section of the Design tab and click on the arrow under Watermark on the far right-hand side. (In Word 2010 and Word 2007, the watermark option was located in the Page Background section of the Page Layout tab.)

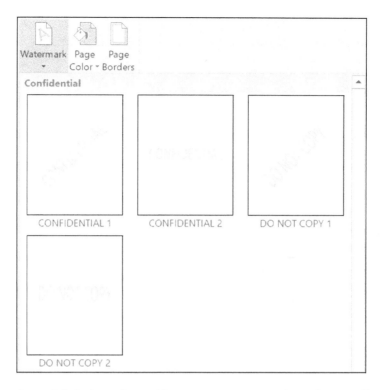

Word provides a number of default options. Above you can see options that say Confidential or Do Not Copy. If you scroll down you'll see options that say Draft, Sample, ASAP, and Urgent.

If you need your watermark to say something else, or you want to change the color or font, or insert an image as your watermark, you can choose the Custom Watermark option at the bottom of the dropdown. This brings up the Printed Watermark dialogue box.

From there you can click on Picture Watermark or Text Watermark and add your image or your text and adjust the font, color, etc. to your liking. When you're done, click Apply.

To remove a watermark, go back to the Watermark option in the Page Background section of the Design tab and choose Remove Watermark from the dropdown menu.

ADD LINE NUMBERING TO A DOCUMENT

The only place I've ever seen line numbering in a document was for interview transcripts or legal briefs, but in case you need it…

To add line numbering to your document go to the Page Layout tab and click on the dropdown next to Line Numbers. You can choose to have continuous line numbering throughout the entire document or have it restart on each page or for each section. (I talk about how to create sections in your document later.)

To specify what number to start numbering with and/or what increments to use for your numbering (so you could start at 10 and go up by 10 instead of it starting at 1 and going up by one each line), click on Line Numbering Options to bring up the Page Setup dialogue box. From there click on Line Numbers to bring up the Line Numbers dialogue box. You can also specify here how far from the text the numbers should be.

You can also bring up that Page Setup dialogue box by going to the File tab, selecting Print, and then clicking on Page Setup at the bottom of the list of options. You can then click on Line Numbers at the bottom of the Layout tab to bring up the Line Numbers dialogue box.

INSERT A SYMBOL

I insert symbols into my documents when I need to use a foreign currency symbol such as the Euro or Pound mark. I've also used it for copyright and trademark symbols as well. (Although Word does have shortcuts for those last two. As mentioned in *Word for Beginners* I've erased the one for copyright in my version of Word because I use (c) too often to have it convert to the copyright symbol every time I type it.)

To insert a symbol into your document, click on the location in your document where you want to insert the symbol and then go to the Symbols section of the Insert tab and click on the Symbol dropdown. (It's on the far right-hand side.) You'll see a selection of recently used symbols and/or commonly used symbols as well as an option for More Symbols. If you click on More Symbols this will bring up the Symbol dialogue box.

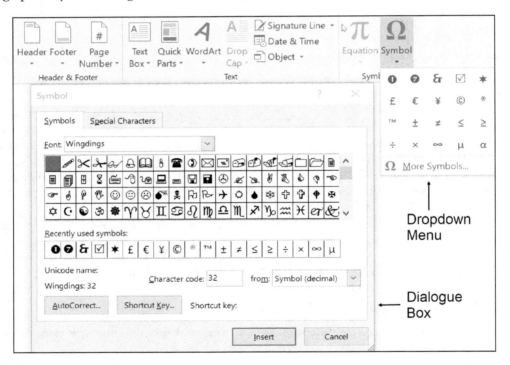

Scroll through the available options until you find the symbol you need. For shapes like mailboxes or folders or two-dimensional arrows, change the Font to one of the Wingdings options since that's where most images and shapes can be found.

Once you find the symbol you want to use, click on it. Next, click on Insert. Word will place the symbol you chose into your document at the location where your cursor was. Once you've inserted a symbol into your document, you can select it and change the font size or color just like you would normal text.

(It appears that at least in my version of Word, you can't change the font which would change the symbol. This is different from how Excel 2013 handles symbols and may be different from how older versions of Word do. So if you insert a symbol into your document be careful about later changing the font because in some versions of Word that may change the symbol to something else.)

Also note that the dialogue box doesn't close after you insert the symbol. You can actually leave it open while you're working if you need to.

ADVANCED FORMATTING

I covered basic formatting like bold, italics, and underline in *Word for Beginners*, but I didn't cover some of the less common formatting options, so let's do that now.

STRIKETHROUGH YOUR TEXT

If you ever want to keep text but place a line through the middle of it as if someone has come along and stricken it out, you can use strikethrough. To do so, select the text, go to the Font section of the Home tab, and choose the strikethrough option. It's the one with the letters abc with a line running through them just to the right of the underline option.

(Back in the good old days before track changes had really caught on, I worked with someone who showed their changes in a document this way. They'd use strikethrough to show the text they wanted deleted. Don't ever do that. Because if you do it that way someone is going to have to go through that document and manually delete all of your strikethroughs. That is not fun. If you run across a document where someone has done this, you can turn off strikethrough in the same way as you add it. Select the text and click on the strikethrough icon in the Font section of the Home tab.)

Anyway. You can also select your text, right-click, choose Format from the dropdown, and then choose Strikethrough from the Effects section of the Font dialogue box. That approach also allows you to choose a double strikethrough option that puts two lines through the text instead of just one.

SUBSCRIPT OR SUPERSCRIPT YOUR TEXT

You may have painful flashbacks to math while we're talking about this and I apologize for that. A subscript is when you move the text so that it's lower than the rest of the text on the line and make it small. A superscript is when you move the text so that it's higher than the rest of the text on the line and also make it small. The best example of a superscript is the notation for a squared number. Remember three squared? It was written as 3^2?

If you ever need to do this (and I have needed to use superscripts when someone accidentally changed the formatting of all footnotes in a document to normal-size text), select the text you want to subscript or superscript and then go to the Font section of the Home tab. The two options are located just below where you choose the font size and just to the right of the strikethrough option.

They're represented by a small bold x with a 2 in the subscript or superscript position, respectively. (Also, if you hold your mouse over each one, Word will tell you what they are and what they do.)

You can also access the subscript or superscript options by selecting your text, right-clicking, and choosing Font from the dropdown menu to bring up the Font dialogue box. The subscript and superscript options are in the Effects section of the Font tab.

They also have Ctrl shortcuts. Subscript is Ctrl + = and superscript is Ctrl + Shift + +. (That second one is holding down the control key, the shift key, and the + key all at the same time.)

PLACE A BOX AROUND YOUR TEXT

This is separate from inserting a table into your document which we'll talk about later. If you just want there to be a box around your text (for a resume, for example), you can click anywhere in the paragraph you want a border around, go to the Paragraph section of the Home tab, click on the Borders dropdown, and choose Outside Borders.

PLACE A LINE ABOVE OR BELOW TEXT

You can also use the Borders dropdown to place a line above and/or below your text. Select the text, go to the Paragraph section of the Home tab, click on the Borders dropdown, and choose Bottom Border, Top Border, or both.

PLACE A COLORED BACKGROUND BEHIND YOUR TEXT (SHADING)

You can also add color behind your text. Although they have a similar appearance, this is different from highlighting your text, because this option has a lot more colors available and can also apply to an entire paragraph of text not just selected word(s).

To apply Shading to your text, click on the paragraph or select the text you want shaded, go to the Paragraph section of the Home tab, click on the arrow next to the Shading image (the paint bucket pouring paint), and choose your color from the dropdown menu.

ADD HYPHENATION TO YOUR DOCUMENT

Hyphenation occurs when a word is continued from the current line onto the next line. This is shown by placing a small dash (called a hyphen) at the end of the first part of the word so that the reader knows that the word continues onto the next line. If you read a lot of books you've probably run across hyphenation and not even realized it.

In a work document or school paper you're not liable to need this. But if you are ever formatting a publication that uses justified paragraphs, you may want to use hyphenation to prevent Word from putting abnormal spaces into your text.

The hyphenation option is located in the Page Setup section of the Page Layout tab. You can choose to automatically or manually hyphenate using the dropdown next to the Hyphenation option. If you want more control, you can open the Hyphenation dialogue box by clicking on Hyphenation Options from the dropdown menu.

If you do choose to use hyphenation, know the rules. Bad hyphenation (e.g., every line in a paragraph hyphenated) is very noticeable.

DISPLAY TEXT IN MULTIPLE COLUMNS

If you look at most magazines or newspapers, you'll see that they use multiple columns on the page. Like this:

This is sample text to show you what multiple columns look like on a page.	You can create a document that has one, two, or three even columns or one where there's a small column to the left or right of your main text.	It can be pretty handy to use if you need to put text elements side-by-side.

You can convert your text into two or three columns using the dropdown menu under Columns in the Page Setup section of the Page Layout tab. All you do is select your text and then choose how many columns you want.

If you click on More Columns in the Columns dropdown, this will bring up a Columns dialogue box which allows you to have up to nine columns on the page and to specify the width of each column separately. It also allows you to place a line between each of the columns.

If you add columns to your document, all of the text will continue down the entire page in the left-most column before moving to the next column on the page and all the way down that column before moving to the next column after that.

If you don't want that—if you want the new column to start with a specific sentence instead—you can use section breaks or column page breaks to force the columns to break where you want them to. (We're going to talk about breaks more in the next section. In the sample above, I used a column page break to force the text into each new column.)

Also, I'll just note here that I tend to use tables for something like this instead of columns. I prefer the level of control I have with tables, but it does require more manual placement of the text than the columns option which can be applied to an entire document in less than a minute.

INSERTING BREAKS

If you want to build more complex documents, page and section breaks are essential.

None of this enter, enter, enter to get down to the next page. Do not do that. As soon as you change your font or font size or make any text edits anywhere in the document, it will all go sideways. Instead use page or section breaks.

Another nice perk of section breaks is they give you the ability to have different headers, footers, columns, and page orientations in different sections of your document. (I have worked at companies that got around this by having each section of a report be a separate document. Once final, the documents were then saved as PDFs and merged together as one document. Or they were just kept as separate standalone documents. But you don't have to do that. Not if you don't want to.)

So page breaks and section breaks. Learn them. They're fantastic.

LOCATION

Page, column, and section breaks can be found in the Page Setup section of the Page Layout tab. If you click on the dropdown menu under Breaks, you'll see that there are multiple options to choose from.

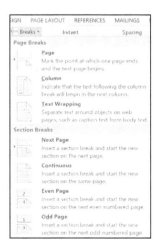

From here you can insert a page break, column break, or section break into your document. If you just want a simple Page Break, you can also go to the Pages section of the Insert tab and click on Page Break from there or use Ctrl + Return to insert a page break into your document.

PAGE BREAKS

When I think of page breaks, I think of stopping where I am on the current page and moving to the top of the next page. For example, I use page breaks at the end of all of my chapters.

The simplest way to insert one is with Ctrl + Return. Or you can go to the Insert tab and click on Page Break under the Pages section. Or, last but not least, and the one I tend to use, you can go to the Page Layout tab, click on Breaks, and then select Page (the first option) from the dropdown menu.

For all three options, you should have your cursor positioned at the point in the document where you want the break to appear, so directly after your last sentence in that section.

(One thing to note: Sometimes Word is strange and when you insert a break at the end of a sentence it will stretch out the last line of text as if trying to justify it. To get rid of this, just go to the end of that sentence and hit enter once. That should return the last line to normal spacing.)

COLUMN BREAKS

I briefly mentioned column breaks above when we were talking about how to display text in multiple columns. A column break allows you to make sure that text you want in a specific column appears in that column. To insert a column break, click into the document at the point where you want the new column to start and then go to the Breaks dropdown menu in the Page Setup section of the Page Layout tab and select Column from the dropdown menu.

SECTION BREAKS

Section breaks are essential for when you want to change the header or footer between parts of your document or for when you want to use a different page orientation or number of columns in different parts of your document. For example, I use them in all of my print books to separate the title page, etc. from the main chapters in the book. I also use them when I have blank pages at the end of a chapter in a non-fiction book. In a business or school setting, you could use section breaks to separate an appendix from a report.

The section break I use is the Next Page option. It's the first one listed under Section breaks and it inserts a break and starts a new section at the top of the next page.

To insert it, do just like you would with a page break. Go to the point in the document where you want the break, go to the Page Setup section of the Page Layout tab, click on the dropdown for Breaks, and choose Next Page.

As you can see in that dropdown, you can also insert a section break in the middle of a page using the continuous section break option. You could use that option for a document where you want to use multiple columns on only one part of the page or where you want the text across columns to split before reaching the bottom of the page. (For example, a page with two separate articles where article A is the first half of the page and article B is the second half of the page.)

You can also set section breaks so that not only do they move to the next page, they move to the next even or odd page. This would be ideal for formatting my non-fiction books, for example, where I want all chapters to start on odd-numbered pages. However, I tried using it in a book I was formatting and it did not work well for me at all. At first it looked great. It inserted a completely blank page for the even-numbered pages at the end of a chapter (which is what I wanted) and started the next chapter on an odd-numbered page. But I then noticed that when I inserted the next section break the one I had already inserted reverted back to a simple section break that just started on the next available page. So I can't recommend (at least in Word 2013) using the odd and even page section break options unless you only have one in your entire document.

(What can I say? I'm brilliant at breaking things other people think work.)

SHOW FORMATTING

Now that we've talked about inserting breaks into your document, it's time to talk about how to see the hidden formatting in a document. This is particularly useful when you're trying to make sure a document with multiple sections, breaks, or numbered lists is formatted correctly.

To see formatting marks in your document, go to the Paragraph section of the Home tab and click on the Paragraph symbol. It's the one with two parallel lines capped with a line that has a bit of a swoosh on the left-hand side.

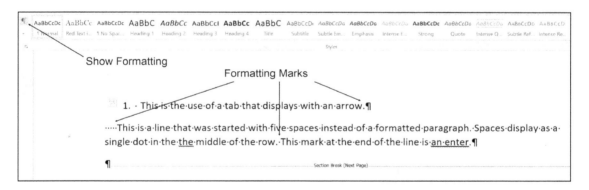

When you click on the symbol, it will change your document so that you can see all the hidden formatting, including your breaks, tabs, and spaces. In the image above a Section Break is visible, along with the notation that it's one that will start the next section on an even page. There's also an arrow next to the number that indicates a tab was used to space the text from the number, and dots to show where spaces are.

When I'm trying to troubleshoot a formatting issue in a document, this is an essential step. This is how I figured out that someone had manually numbered entries in the midst of an automatically numbered list. Instead of seeing a space, the number, a little arrow, and then text (like above) I was seeing dots that indicated spaces, then the number, then more dots, and then text.

So if you have formatting that doesn't look right, turn on show formatting to see if any of your entries are formatted differently from those around them.

Also, a warning. If you have a line of text that is almost to the edge of the page and there's a page or section break at the end of that line, it will be very difficult to see it. When this happens to me, I go to the end of the line and hit enter to see if there's a break that I'm not seeing. Once I'm done working on that page, I remove the extra return.

HEADERS AND FOOTERS
(INTERMEDIATE VERSION)

In *Word for Beginners*, we covered the very basics of adding a header or footer. (Go to the Insert tab and choose Header, Footer, or Page Number from the Header & Footer section and then choose the position on the page where you want it to be.) But you can do a lot more with headers and footers than that.

Let's cover some simple options and then work our way up to making things really complicated.

OPENING A HEADER OR FOOTER

Most of what we're about to talk about requires that you be in the header or footer of the document. When you insert a header or footer, you're automatically taken to the header or the footer. But after you've inserted them and returned to your main document, they're in a separate section of the document. To edit them, you need to go back there. To do so, you can double-click on where the header or footer is located. This works very well with the header section, but not as well with the footer section. Or, you can right-click on the header or footer section and it should bring up a small box that says Edit Header or Edit Footer. Click on that and you'll be in the header or footer. From there, treat the text just like you would with any other text in your document.

To exit the header or footer and return to your main body text, use the Esc key or double-click in the main body of the document.

DIFFERENT FIRST PAGE HEADER/FOOTER/PAGE NUMBER

If you open most books you'll see that there isn't a header on the first page of any chapter. It's blank. But then the rest of the chapter does have a header. And if you have a report with a cover page, chances are you won't want a header on that cover page. So how do you do this?

First, insert a header. Now, look at the menu bar above your document. You should see a Design tab with the label Header & Footer Tools. Like this:

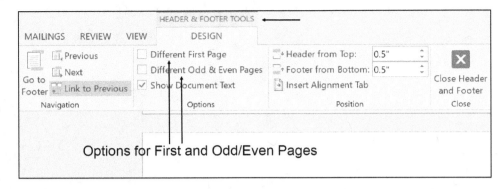

Options for First and Odd/Even Pages

If you look in the center of that tab, you'll see a section called Options and a box labeled Different First Page. If you check the box, Word will treat the first page of any section differently from the other pages in the section.

Be careful when using this one, because if you're on the first page of the section, that header you enter is only going to show on that page. If you're on a different page of the section and you make edits to the header, they won't be reflected on the first page. So always be sure to check your headers on ALL pages when you're done.

Also, at least in my version of Word, making that choice applies to both the header and footer. So I had a document with text in the header and page numbering in the footer. When I chose "different first page" for the header section that also removed my page numbering from that first page. I had to open the footer and choose Page Number under the Header & Footer Tools to put a page number on that first page.

And don't worry if it takes a few tries to get your headers and footers looking the way you want them to. I've been doing this for years and I still make mistakes. Remember Ctrl + Z (Undo) is your friend.

Also, with a really complex document that has lots of different sections and headers/footers, I would save a version before you start, just in case. Sometimes it's easier to start over rather than try to undo everything you've done wrong.

DIFFERENT ODD AND EVEN PAGES

I don't recall ever using this with a business report or school paper, but I do use it with book formatting. Pick up a book from your shelf and you're liable to see that most books have the title or current chapter name on one page and the author name on the facing page throughout the main body of the book.

How do you do this?

First, insert your header or footer. Next, click on Different Odd & Even Pages in the Options section of the Header & Footer Tools Design tab. Similar to how it worked above, once you make that choice, any changes you make to an odd-numbered page will only apply to your odd-numbered pages and any changes you make to an even-numbered page will only apply to your even-numbered pages.

It gets really fun when you have both the Different First Page box checked and the Different Odd & Even Pages box checked, because that means you have three separate headers and footers per section.

If you're going to be doing this a lot, it's a good idea to build a template that you can work with each time. (For example, for paperback formatting CreateSpace provides templates with sample text. If you ever use Word to format a book, I'd highly recommend using them.)

HEADERS AND FOOTERS AND SECTION BREAKS

The choices we just discussed allow for some pretty sophisticated formatting without ever requiring a section break. But if you have any blank pages in your document (say between chapters or sections) or if you need to have different headers or footers (say in an appendix), then you're going to need to combine the use of section breaks with the use of headers and footers.

We already talked about how to insert a section break. That's very simple. (Page Layout tab, Breaks dropdown menu.) And the nice thing about Word is that it defaults to continuing your page numbering as well as your headers and footers across sections.

If you look in the Headers & Footers Tools Design tab you'll see a Link to Previous option that is already selected by default. This means that, unless you do something to change it, your header and footer in this section are going to be the same as your header and footer in your surrounding sections.

So, if for example you inserted a section break to start a new chapter, then you likely don't have to do anything else. Word will treat the first page of that new chapter the same as it did the first page of the last chapter and will keep the header and footer settings and contents you had set for that prior section.

If, however, you insert a section break because you want to change something in the header or footer compared to the sections around it, then you're going to need to unlink the section before you make your changes. Otherwise, you will change all sections in your document at the same time. For example, when I insert a section break to create a blank page on an even-numbered page at the end of a chapter, I make sure the Link to Previous option is no longer selected before I delete the page number at the bottom of the page.

It's a best practice to always scroll up and down about three pages when you make an edit like this to make sure you didn't delete the header or footer on another page. It's amazing how easy it is to delete something on page five and also delete something on page eight. (Remember, in any given section you could have three different headers and footers, so a change you make on page five may not affect the headers and footers on pages six and seven, but could still affect the headers and footers on page eight.)

ADDING DATE AND/OR TIME TO YOUR HEADER OR FOOTER

This one is actually pretty simple. To insert the date and/or time into your header or footer, go to the location where you want to insert it (the header or footer), and then go to the Header & Footer Tools Design tab. In the Insert section click on Date & Time. This will bring up a Date & Time dialogue box. Choose the date and/or time format you want.

If you want the date and time to update so that it always displays the current time, be sure to check the box that says so. (Just be sure that's what you really want. I can't count the number of memos I've seen where someone used the automatic date option and shouldn't have. Instead of the memo being dated the day it was actually written and finalized, the memo updated to the current date each time it was opened. That may not seem like a big issue, but if you're writing a memo to a file to document when an important event occurred it can become a very, very big issue.)

ADDING DOCUMENT INFORMATION TO YOUR HEADER OR FOOTER

You can also have the header or footer include certain document information such as the Author, File Name, File Path, or Document Title.

To do this, navigate to where you want to this information to be (the header or footer), and then go to the Header & Footer Tools Design tab and click on the dropdown for Document Info in the Insert section. You can choose Author, File Name, File Type, and Document Title from the dropdown menu. If you want to include other information about the document, click on Field in the dropdown menu. That will open a dialogue box with a number of options to choose from.

All of the document information fields are dynamic fields, so will update as the information changes.

EDITING HEADER/FOOTER POSITION OR FONT

By default in Word 2013, the header and footer are positioned .5" from the top and bottom of the page. If you want to change that setting, it's in the Position section of the Header & Footer Tools Design tab.

To change the font, font size, or color of the text in your header or footer, it works just like normal text formatting. Select the text you want to change and use the options in the Font section of the Home tab. You can also select the text you want to change and then right-click and pull up the Font dialogue box.

STYLES

Alright. Time to discuss a formatting option that is much easier to work with than paragraph-by-paragraph formatting but that requires a little bit of effort to set up: Styles.

Styles allow you to create a pre-set paragraph format. You get to specify the font, font size, line spacing, text color, whether the paragraph is indented or not, if there's a space between that paragraph and those around it, etc. You can then apply this style to every single paragraph in your document so that they all look the same.

When I format an ebook or paperback, I use two main styles. One is for the first paragraph of a section and has no indent. The other is for all other paragraphs in the document. It's identical to the first style except the paragraph is indented. I will also sometimes use a style for chapter headings. (The CreateSpace template I mentioned previously uses one for chapter headings. In ebooks I usually use Heading 1 for chapter headings.)

Word by default uses a style called Normal. In my version of Word that style uses the Calibri font in an 11 point size with left-aligned paragraphs, a line spacing of 1.08, and a space of 8 points after each paragraph. It also includes widow and orphan control.

Word also provides a number of other Styles that you can choose from. You can see them in the Styles section of the Home tab. Here are the first six:

Each one is formatted to show what it looks like when used and you can right-click on any style and choose Modify to see exactly what formatting it uses. I generally don't like the default styles. I don't need blue italicized text and if I'm going to bold something I can do that with Ctrl + B. The only default styles that really matter to me are Heading 1 and Heading 2. This is because I use them for document navigation while I'm writing and I sometimes use them for inserting a table of contents.

The real power in using styles is creating your own. It only takes setting them up once and then you can apply them in all of your documents going forward to create a consistent appearance both within the document in question and across all of your documents.

The easiest way to create a custom style is to take one paragraph and format it exactly how you want it. Select the paragraph and then click on the arrow with a bar at the bottom of the Styles box on the right-hand side to expand the Styles selections. This will bring up the option to Create a Style.

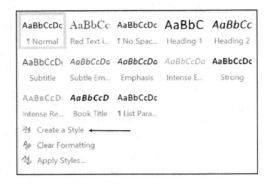

Click on that option and name your style. When you click on OK the new style will be added to your list of style options, generally in the first row of choices. If it turns out the style that was created wasn't exactly what you wanted, you can right-click on the style and choose Modify. This will bring up the Modify Style dialogue box.

The most common attributes you'll want to change are included on the main screen of the dialogue box, but you can also click on the Format option in the bottom left corner and bring up dialogue boxes for font, paragraph, etc.

Be careful if you leave a style linked to the Normal style like I have in this example. Any changes you make to the Normal style may also impact this style. (A reason I don't modify my Normal style.)

Also, you can choose to either have the style you've created available in only this document or to make it available in all other documents.

(I'm weird so I limit a style to the current document and then use Format Painter to transfer the style to a new document when it's needed. To use Format Painter to bring a style into a new document, select the paragraph in the old document that has the style you want, click on Format Painter, go to your new document, and select a paragraph in the new document where you want to apply the style. This should add the style to your style menu and change the formatting of the text you selected.)

To apply a style from the style menu to text it's as simple as clicking into the paragraph that you want to have the style and then clicking on the style. If you hover your mouse over a style, the text you've selected will change to the new style but it won't remain the new style unless you click on the style.

If you want to convert text of one style to another style, right-click on the name of the current style and choose Select All from the dropdown. Once Word has done that—it may take a bit if it's a long document—click on the new style you want to apply to those paragraphs.

You can also right-click on a style and choose Select All and then modify the style. The changes you make to the style will apply to all instances of the style as long as you've selected them. (It isn't automatic that changes to a style apply to all paragraphs that already used that style.)

INSERT IMAGES

Time to talk about something that's pretty straightforward: How to insert an image into your document.

First, go to the place in your document where you want to insert the image. Next, go to the Illustrations section of the Insert tab and click on Pictures.

By default, Word is going to open into the Pictures folder of your user account. If the file for the image you want to insert into your document is somewhere else on your computer, you can navigate to that location. Once you've found your file, click on it and then click on Insert. The image should now appear in your document at the location you selected.

If you want to move the image to a new location within your document, you can click on it and use Ctrl + X to cut it from its current location and Ctrl + V to paste it into the new location. If you want to make edits to the image you can click on it and then use the options that appear in the Picture Tools Format tab.

SIZE

The most common adjustment I make to an image I've inserted into my document is to change its size. When you click on an image you've inserted into your document, you'll be able to see the Picture Tools Format tab. On the right-hand side you can see the current size of the image. In the screenshot above, the image I inserted was 4.73" by 6.49". To change that, you can either use the arrows on the right-hand side of the numbers or, what I do more often, just click into one of the boxes and enter the size you want.

So, for example, in a document like this one, I might change the width of that photo to 4.75" to align it to the size of my paragraphs.

Any adjustment you make to one measure (height or width) will automatically adjust the other measure to keep the overall image proportional.

If you want more options to work with, including allowing an adjustment to just the height or just the width or sizing an image as a proportion of the page, you can click on the expansion arrow in the bottom right corner of the Size section and this will bring up the Format Picture dialogue box.

If I just have one image in a document that I need to resize, so I'm not worried about a precise width or height, I'll often just click on the image and then click on one of the black boxes in the corner of the image and drag towards the center (to make the image smaller) or away from the center (to make the image bigger). If you drag from one of the boxes in the corner, the image will resize proportionately. You can also click on one of the black boxes in the center of each side if you just want to change the width or the height, but be careful because that can distort your image.

Also know that increasing the size of an image is generally not recommended. Your image will tend to blur.

CROPPING

If you want to trim off part of an image, this is called cropping. (I often crop photos, but I usually do it outside of Word, most often in PowerPoint.) You can easily crop images within Word by right-clicking on the image and choosing the Crop option or by going to the Size section of the Picture Tools Format tab and clicking on Crop.

When you do so, you'll see the little crop image next to your mouse (two right angles facing opposite directions that overlap). If you then left-click and drag from any of the little black boxes along the edges of the image, this will crop that section of the image away. By clicking in the boxes in the corner and dragging at a diagonal, you can crop in two directions at once.

(Word's cropping works a little differently than the cropping option in PowerPoint, which is where I normally do my cropping. In my current version of Word when I have crop enabled and I click and drag, Word automatically crops the image. In PowerPoint when I crop it shows me where I've cropped to, but doesn't crop the image until I've hit Esc. I prefer the PowerPoint approach because it allows me to fine-tune exactly where I want to crop my image. YMMV.)

BORDERS

The next most common adjustment I make to images is to add a border around the edge. Especially if you're dealing with an image that has any whitespace along the edge, adding a border can help to distinguish the image.

To add a border to an image, right-click on the image and choose Borders and Shading from the dropdown menu. This will bring up the Borders dialogue box.

I usually place a simple Box border around the image by selecting Box and then clicking OK. You can also adjust the size or color of the line if you want, but I usually don't.

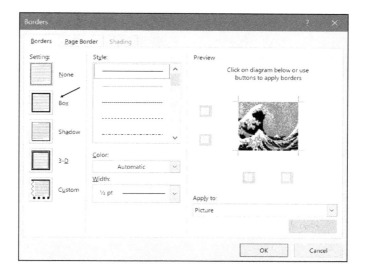

POSITION

I make my life very simple by inserting images on their own line. So as you'll see in this book, there's text, then there's an image, and then there's more text. But you don't have to do it that way. Especially if you have a small image, you may instead want the image and some of your text on the same line. This is done through the Position option in the Arrange section of the Picture Tools Format tab. You have ten choices:

The one I use is In Line With Text. As you can see in the sample, that has the image on its own line. The nine text wrapping options allow you to place your image in one of nine locations on the page (top left, top center, top right, middle left, middle center, middle right, bottom left, bottom center, and bottom right) and then have the text wrap around the image. You can see what each option will look like before you decide by clicking on your image and then holding your cursor over each of the choices.

If you are going to have text alongside an image, you may also need to use the options in the Wrap Text dropdown in the Arrange section of the Picture Tools Format tab. This option dictates how the text will be positioned in relation to an image.

In the same way that you could see how each option would look with the Position dropdown menu, you can move your cursor over each of the Wrap Text options to see how it'll look before you choose the option you want. This is very much an aesthetic adjustment, so you're just going to have to try the different options to see what combination of position and wrapped text create the look you want. (And be careful of adjusting fonts or image size after you've made you choice since that will change how everything works together.)

I will also add that using the Behind Text and In Front of Text options is not something I would recommend, because of the legibility issue. Unless you're working with a mostly transparent image (like a background logo, for example) either the image or the text won't be fully visible.

Also, if you do choose to wrap your text around your image, be sure to read the text when you're done. For example, I have the below photo set to a top center position with square wrap text. It may be hard to see, but the text lines continued from one side of the image to the other so that someone reading that paragraph would have to read across the image on every single line. That's not what I'd expect to find as a reader.

This is sample text. We're going photograph so you can see how going to have to make this picture so after I type this I'm going to  to place it around this this all works, but we're also smaller or else it'll just look silly, shrink that photo down to size.

ADJUSTING THE APPEARANCE OF YOUR IMAGE

I'm not going to dive too deep into this one but I will mention that Word does have options that let you change the appearance of an image you've imported into your document. If you look on the Picture Tools Format tab, on the left-hand side there is an entire section called Adjust that includes settings for Brightness, Contrast, and Color. You can also Rotate your photo in the Arrange section. (So if it imported sideways, you can fix that.)

As with the Position and Wrap Text options above, you can hover your arrow over any of the options in the dropdowns to see what they'll look like before you apply them. If you do end up clicking on an option and not liking it, remember Ctrl + Z (Undo) is your friend.

INSERT A TABLE OF CONTENTS

For business reports, I've often needed a table of contents. And while it may be tempting to just build one yourself, you don't have to and it's probably a better idea to have Word do it for you. If you have Word build it, you can then refresh the table of contents when you're done editing your document and all section names and page numbers will automatically update. (Much better than having to manually check that each page number is correct, something I've had to do in the past.)

In order to have Word generate a table of contents for you, you need to apply the Heading 1, Heading 2, etc. styles to your section headers and any sub-section headers that you want included in the table of contents. If you've done that, than inserting a table of contents is very easy.

I generally only use Heading 1 and Heading 2 in my table of contents, but if you do need more levels than that, you can use them. (If you apply the Heading 1 and Heading 2 styles to text in your document, Word will automatically add the style for Heading 3 to your styles menu options. At least it does in my version.)

Assuming you've already applied your styles to the headers in your document, go to the place in the document where you want your table of contents. Now go to the References tab and on the left-hand side click on the arrow under Table of Contents in the Table of Contents section.

You can either choose from one of the three provided options or you can choose to create a custom table of contents.

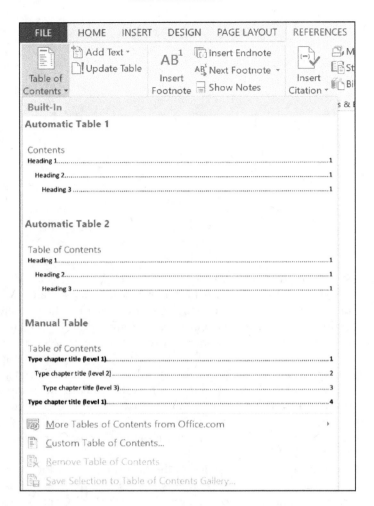

For ebooks I choose to create a custom table of contents because I don't want page numbers included. For business reports, I can usually use one of the default formats.

Let's look at the custom format for a minute:

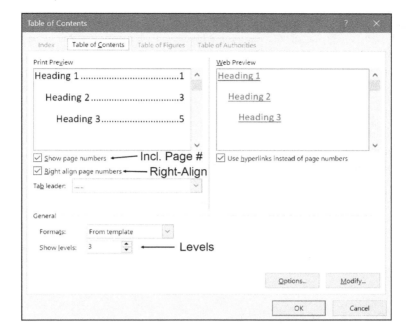

If you don't want to include page numbers, uncheck the Show Page Numbers box.

If you only want to show the main header level, but your document used heading 2 or heading 3, you can limit the number of levels included in the table of contents by changing the dropdown next to Show Levels to 1. (If you want to only display a certain number of levels you can adjust this number to any number between 1 and 9.)

The Tab Leader setting determines what type of line (if any) will display between the heading text and the page number. (If applicable.)

By default, the page numbers will be displayed on the far right-hand side and aligned. You can turn this off by unchecking the Right Align Page Numbers box, although if you do be sure to look at the preview. (I think it looks horrid when you turn that off.)

Once you've customized your settings, click on OK and Word will insert your table of contents into your document. You can then edit it manually just like you would any other text. I've changed fonts or bolding, for example. But if you do that, keep in mind that any changes you made will be lost if anyone ever refreshes the table of contents.

(You can change the overall settings for your table of contents by choosing custom table of contents and then going to Modify. It will show each level of the table of contents and you can click there to change the settings if you want them to be permanent. Most of the changes I've ever had to make were minor enough I just manually edited the table because that was much simpler to do.)

If you make changes in your document after creating your table of contents, like fixing typos or changing the name of a section, right-click on the table of contents and choose Update Field from the dropdown. You'll then be given the choice to just update page numbers or to update the whole thing.

(You can also go to the Reference tab and in the Table of Contents section click on Update Table. It will take you to the same Update Table of Contents dialogue box that using the dropdown menu does.)

One more thing: If you hadn't applied the Heading 1, Heading 2, etc. styles to the sections you wanted to include in your table of contents, you can do that after you've created your table of contents. Find the header you want included in your table of contents, select it, and go to the Table of Contents section of the Reference tab. Click on Add Text and choose which level of the table of contents you want the text added to.

This will change the formatting of the selected text to match the Heading style for that table of contents level and will add it to the table as well. (You're only going to be able to choose a heading level that corresponds to the ones you've included in your table of contents. So if you said two levels that's all you'll be able to choose from under Add Text. If you said four levels, you'll have four choices.)

In order to see the newly-added text in your table of contents, you will need to refresh the table of contents when you're done.

TABLES:
INSERTING

A table is essentially a grid of spaces. It can have a range of spaces across a row (one, two, three, four, five, etc.) and any number of rows you want. Tables are useful for providing a structure to information that you want to provide your reader. As you've already seen, there are bulleted lists and numbered lists and the option to split your text into columns, but I find tables are the most granular way to control exactly where text appears on the page. (Which isn't to say that I don't use numbered or bulleted lists. I use them all the time. But when I really need precision in terms of how items are spaced, etc. I will sometimes turn to tables.)

So. Let's talk about how to insert a basic table into your document.

First, go to the Insert tab. Next, find the Tables section on the left-hand side and click on the dropdown arrow under Table. Use your mouse to select the number of columns and rows you want in your table by hovering your mouse over the first square on the top left and then moving it to the right and down until you've selected the desired number of columns and rows. Once you have that desired number of rows and columns selected, click on the last cell and Word will insert a table into your document that has the number of columns and rows you selected.

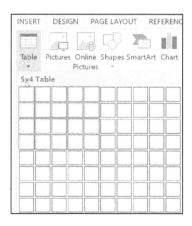

If you'd prefer, you can also insert a table into a document by going to the Tables section of the Insert tab, clicking on the arrow under Table, and choosing Insert Table from the dropdown menu. This brings up the Insert Table dialogue box where you can specify the exact number of columns and rows you want.

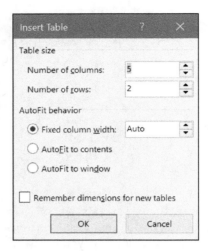

In newer versions of Word you also have the option to insert an Excel spreadsheet or use one of a handful of Quick Tables. Personally, I don't use either of those options. When I want to insert a table I want to format it to my tastes and the Quick Tables options aren't even close to what I would choose. And embedding an Excel file in your Word file can be more tricky than it's worth. (I've done so in PowerPoint before and it can get a little messy.) But they are two more options if you want to try them.

And don't worry if you insert a table and then decide you need it to have more rows or more columns or the columns aren't the width you want them to be. In the next section we'll talk about how to take that basic table you inserted and format it to be exactly what you want.

TABLES:
STRUCTURE

Once you've inserted a table into your document, chances are you'll want to format it. There are many, many options for formatting a table, so let's walk through them.

COLUMN WIDTH

When you insert a table chances are the columns will have the same width and you'll want to adjust that. You have a number of options for doing so.

First, you can place your cursor over the line between two columns. Your cursor should turn into something that looks like two parallel lines with arrows pointing to the left and the right. (You'll probably only be able to see the arrows since the parallel lines will be lined up with the line separating the two columns.) Once your cursor looks like this, you can left-click on the line between the two columns and drag the line to the left or the right to change the width of the column. This will change the width of two columns at once since the other column divider lines will stay stationary.

Second, you can right click into a cell in the column you want to change and choose Table Properties from the dropdown menu. This will bring up the Table Properties dialogue box. From there go to the Column tab and change your column by entering an exact width for that column. (You can do this for all columns at once by selecting the whole table or an entire row in the table and then adjusting the value for column width. This does mean, of course, that they'll all have the same column width.)

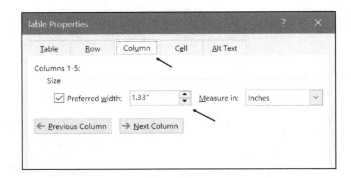

Third, you can go to the Table Tools Layout tab which should be an option once you click on some part of the table. In the Cell Size section, you can change the value for the column you're in by changing the Width value. (You can change all columns at once by selecting the whole table and changing the value, but if you only select one row and use this option it will only change the column widths for that selected row, not the entire table.)

Fourth, if you have text that you've entered into a cell, you can have Word AutoFit the width of the cell to the text you've entered by going to the Table Tools Layout tab and clicking on the dropdown arrow under AutoFit in the Cell Size section. From there choose AutoFit Contents. (Be careful if you do this and only have text in one cell, because all of your other columns will also be adjusted, but to the smallest possible width.)

ROW HEIGHT

Your options for adjusting the height of a row in your table are mostly the same as for changing the column width, although there will be some row heights you can't achieve because Word forces a minimum row height based upon font size.

First, you can place your cursor over the line dividing any rows in the table and left-click and drag to your desired height.

Second, you can right-click on any cell in a row and choose Table Properties to bring up the Table Properties dialogue box. From there go to the Row tab and input your desired row height.

Or third, you can use the Table Tools Layout tab to specify the row height by changing the number for Height in the Cell Size section.

(AutoFit is not an option for row height. It only works on column width.)

Whichever method you use, be sure to look at the table after you're done, because if you tried to specify a row height that was smaller than Word allowed, it won't change even though the number looks like it has. (To get around this, at least to a certain extent if there isn't text in that row, you can manually change the font size for the cells in that row to 1 point.)

TABLE WIDTH

An attribute of tables that I often change is the overall width of the table. To do this, right-click on the table and select Table Properties. When the Table Properties dialogue box comes up, go to the Table tab and click on the box for Preferred Width under Size and then specify the width you want for the table.

You can also go to the right-hand side of the table, hover your mouse over that outside column line until you see the two parallel lines with arrows on either side, and then left-click and drag until you have the table width you want. Just know that you may run into issues with this approach if you're trying to make a table smaller, because you can only drag so far before Word stops you because you've reached the minimum width for the last column in the table. (You can then change that column's width and keep going, but it turns out to be a multi-step process most of the time. It's still the way I usually do it, though.)

Another option if you want the table to be the width of the page is to use AutoFit. Click on the table, go to the Cell Size section of the Table Tools Layout tab, click on the dropdown arrow under AutoFit, and choose AutoFit Window.

MOVING A TABLE

If you have a table that isn't the entire width of the page, chances are you'll need to move it to where you want it on that line. To do this, place your cursor over the table. You should now see a square box appear off the side of the top left corner of the table. It will have arrows pointing in all four cardinal directions. Left-click on that box and drag the table to where you want it. (This also works for dragging the table to another location in the document.)

If you want to move the table to a different document or a significantly different location in your current document, you can also right-click on the box in the top-left corner, choose Copy or Cut from the dropdown menu, go to the new location, and Paste.

DELETING THE CONTENTS OF A TABLE

To delete the contents of a table, you can select all of the cells in the table and then use the Delete key. The table will remain, but all of the text will be removed.

DELETING A CELL, ROW, COLUMN, OR ENTIRE TABLE

To delete an entire table, you can select all of the cells in the table and use the Backspace key. This will delete both the contents within the table as well as the table itself.

To delete a table, you can also right-click on the box in the top left corner of the table and choose Delete Table from the dropdown menu.

To delete a row, select the row you want to delete and then use the Backspace key. This will show you the Delete Cells dialogue box. Choose to Delete Entire Row and click OK.

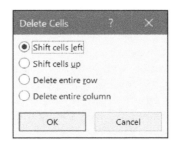

To delete a column, select the column you want to delete and use the Backspace key. It should delete automatically.

To delete a cell, row, or column, you can right-click in a cell in the table and choose Delete Cells from the dropdown menu. This will bring up the Delete Cells dialogue box (above). From there you can choose to delete the individual cell or the entire row or column. If you delete just a cell, other cells in that row or column will have to shift to fill the space, so be careful because deleting that one cell may rearrange your information in ways you don't like.

To delete cells, columns, rows, or tables, you can also go to the Table Tools Layout tab and click on the Delete option in the Rows and Columns section. In the dropdown you can then choose to delete a cell, row, column, or the entire table.

INSERTING A CELL, ROW, OR COLUMN

If you need to add a cell, row, or column to your table there are a number of ways to do so.

To insert a cell, click into an existing cell in the table that is where you want to insert the cell. Right-click and on the dropdown menu hold your mouse over the Insert option and then choose Insert Cells from the new dropdown menu that should appear. You'll then see the Insert Cells dialogue box. You can either choose to shift cells to the right or down to make room for the new cell.

To insert a row or column, you can also click into an existing cell in the table that is where you want the new row or column, right-click, hover your mouse over the Insert option and then choose one of the insert row or column choices on the second dropdown menu.

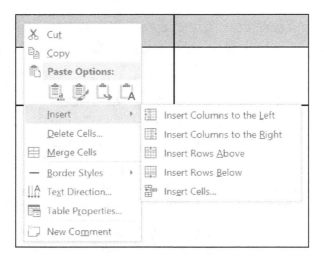

A quick way to insert a new row at the bottom of an existing table is to go to the last cell in the table (the one in the bottom right-hand corner) and then use the Tab key.

Another way to insert a new row or column is by using the Table Tools Layout tab and going to the Rows & Columns section. Click into the spot in your table where you want to insert the new row or column and then choose Insert Above or Insert Below for a row or Insert Left or Insert Right for a column.

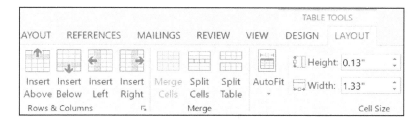

To insert multiple rows or columns at once, select multiple rows or columns in your table and then choose one of the insert options. If you select three rows and choose to insert more rows, it will insert three more rows. If you select two columns and choose to insert columns, it will insert two more columns.

SPLITTING OR MERGING CELLS

One of the nice features when working with tables in Word is that you can split cells. This means that different rows in your table can have a different number of columns in them. So if you want to put a row of labels at the top of your table where each label covers multiple columns, you can do that.

Like this:

Book Information		
Title	Pub Date	Pages

See how in this table I've created a first row that is just one cell that says Book Information, and then on the next row I have three separate columns of book information: Title, Pub Date, and Pages?

If you already have an existing table with the number of columns you need, you can insert a new row at the top and merge cells to create the header in that first row.

One way to merge the cells is to select all of the cells in the first row and then go to the Table Tools Layout tab and choose Merge Cells from the Merge section. (The Merge Cells option only shows as available when you have more than one cell selected.)

The other option is to select all of the cells in the row, right-click, and choose Merge Cells from the dropdown menu.

(Unlike in Excel, if you merge two cells with text in them, Word will keep the text from both cells in the new merged cell.)

What if instead you've built a table like this but now want to add a new column? You can't just insert a column because you have that header row with the merged cells. In that case, you can split cells in one of your existing columns to form a new column.

Using the table pictured above, I could select the cell that says Title as well as all of the cells in the column below it. (Note I'm not selecting any cell from the first row of the table.) I would then go to the Table Tools Layout tab and choose Split Cells from the Merge section. This brings up the Split Cells dialogue box that allows me to tell Word how many rows and columns to split the cells into.

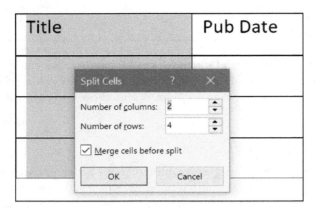

In this case, because I want two columns out of the one that I have now, I say two columns and five rows.

If you already have text in more than just the first cell you've chosen to split, uncheck the box that says "Merge cells before split." Also, if you do have text in the cells you're splitting check after you split the cells that your text in the cells is where you think it should be.

You can also split an individual cell by right-clicking and choosing Split Cells, but that only works on one cell at a time.

SPLIT TABLE

You can take an existing table and split it into two tables. Usually this won't be necessary because, as we'll discuss in a moment, with large tables you can format them so the top row(s) repeat on each page. But I do use this sometimes when formatting the table of contents in my print books. It gives me the most control over how a table of contents that continues onto a second page appears.

To take an existing table and split it, select the row that you want to be the first row in the second table. Next, click on Split Table in the Merge section of the Table Tools Layout tab. Instead of one table with continuous rows, you'll now see two tables that were split apart at the row you selected. In the image below, I had selected row 3 before using Split Table.

1		
2		
3		

4		
5		

(I should also note that Split Table did not want to work for me when I was using a table that had a different number of columns in each row, so if you think you're going to split a table, try to do so before you split your columns.)

SPACING BETWEEN CELLS

You can also format a table so that there are spaces between each of the cells in the table. Like this:

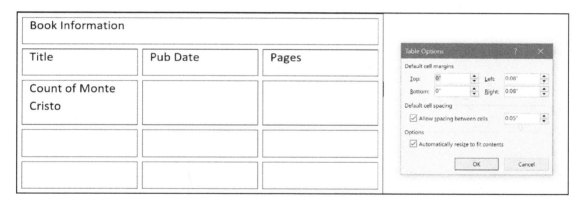

See how there's space between all of the cells in this table instead of just a line?

To do this, click on your table, go to the Alignment section of the Table Tools Layout tab, and click on Cell Margins. This will bring up the Table Options dialogue box. If you click on Allow Spacing Between Cells you can specify a space that's wide enough to be visible like I did here.

You can also do this by right-clicking on your table, choosing Table Properties from the dropdown menu, and then clicking on Options on the Table tab.

TABLES:
FORMATTING

Alright. We've talked about how to build your table. Now it's time to talk about all the formatting that you can do within the cells of the table. This is probably where I spend most of my time when I'm working on tables.

TABLE STYLES

If you don't want to mess with specific formatting for your table, but do want it to look like more than a set of generic boxes, the simplest way to do that is to apply a Table Style to your table. Table Styles can be found in the Table Tools Design tab in the Table Styles section. The first few entries are just basic black and white options with some lines made invisible or with some gray shading to separate lines. If you click on the arrow with a line in the bottom right corner, though, you can expand the list of options to see a number of additional options, some of which use colors.

To apply a table style, click on your table and then click on the style you want. This will overwrite any line or background fill or font color you already applied to the table. (Which is what we're about to discuss.)

To the left of the available styles are six checkboxes. Check these based upon whether you have a header row, total row, or want special formatting on your first column or last column. Depending on the style, that will mean different things for those rows and columns, usually bolding or color differences, but also sometimes differences in the border lines.

FONT, FONT SIZE, FONT COLOR, ETC.

If you want to change the font, font size, text color, add bold or italics to text in a cell, or any other basic text formatting, you do so in the same way that you would format text in other parts of your document.

For the entire table, click on the box in the top left corner to select all cells in the table first. If it's for specific cells, select those cells. If it's for specific text, select the word(s) you want to format. Next, go to the Font section of the Home tab and make your formatting selections.

Be careful with changing the font or font size, because the table will automatically resize itself to accommodate your text to make sure it remains visible.

BACKGROUND FILL (SHADING)

I use the first row of most tables as a header row that contains labels for each column. To distinguish this row from the rows that have the content, I often will color the cells in the row. Like this:

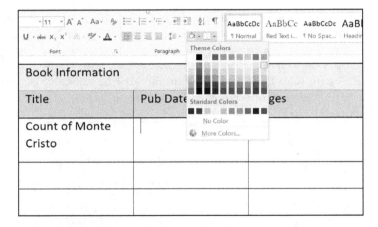

The first two rows have shading to designate them as header rows and then the actual data the table is providing starts on row three.

To add shading to cells, select the cells where you want to add shading, go to the Paragraph section of the Home tab, and click on the arrow next to the paint bucket on the bottom right-hand side (that says Shading if you hold your mouse over it) and choose a color from the dropdown menu.

There are seventy colors you can choose from in Word 2013. If that's not enough (for example, you need to use a corporate color), you can click on More Colors at the bottom. This will bring up the Colors dialogue box. From there you can either choose a color from the honeycomb of colors on the Standard tab or you can go to the Custom tab and enter the RGB values for the color you need. (My last client had a corporate color palette and when they published the corporate colors guideline it include the RGB values for each of the corporate colors, making them easy to incorporate into a document.)

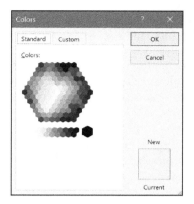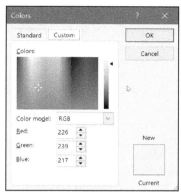

If you don't want to use the Home tab options, you can also click on Shading from the Table Styles section of the Table Tools Design tab.

Or you can open the Borders and Shading dialogue box from the Paragraph section of the Home tab by clicking on the Borders dropdown and choosing Borders and Shading and then going to the Shading tab.

TABLE LINE STYLES, WEIGHT, AND COLOR

Another aspect of a table that you might want to adjust is the appearance of the lines that form the table. For example, in the table of contents for my print books I use a table, but I don't want those lines visible, so for those tables I change the line style to No Border. I've also had situations where I wanted a thicker outer border around a table and then thinner lines within the table.

To change the lines on a table that you've already created, first go to the Borders section of the Table Tools Design tab and choose the line style, weight (thickness), and color you want.

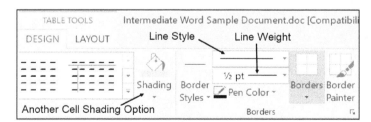

Next, select the cells where you want to apply that line style, weight, and color. (If it's all, just select the whole table.) Now, go back to the Borders section of the Table Tools Design tab and click what border lines you want to place around those cells. (If it's all borders then it's the All Borders option. If it's just the outside edge of the table, then it's the Outside Borders option.)

You can use more than one style/weight/color on the lines in your table, but if you do so be careful about the order in which you format your cells. For example, if I wanted a thicker outside border, I would apply the inside border formatting to all cells first and then do the outside border second. Because if I did the outside border first and then tried to format the inside borders differently, it would take me more steps since I couldn't just use the All Border option to format the cells along the edge of the table.

You can also apply more than one *type* of border to a specific cell. So you can choose top border and bottom border for the same cell, for example.

And don't forget that you need to set your line formatting first and then choose the cells and type of border to apply. If you don't do that you'll be applying the existing line formatting to your cells. (Don't worry if you do get it out of order. It'll be pretty obvious and then you just fix it. I've done it a number of times myself.)

If it sounds a little too complicated to you to figure out how to get that line on the bottom of the second cell from the right to be formatted in a specific way using the Border dropdown menu, then try the Border Painter instead. As above, you need to set the way you want the line to look in terms of weight, color, and style before you use the Border Painter. Once you've done that, go to the Borders section of the Table Tools Design tab and click on the Border Painter option.

Your cursor should turn into a little paintbrush. Next, click on the lines in your table that you want to format that way and Word will apply the format to just that specific line in that cell. (Which means it's a much slower option than using the Borders dropdown if you're trying to format a number of cells.)

You can also choose from a set of pre-defined line styles that are available either in the Borders section of the Table Tools Design tab under Border Styles, or by right-clicking on your table and choosing Border Styles from the dropdown menu. Both options will bring up a set of line colors/weights/styles that you can choose from and then the Border Painter tool that will allow you to apply the style to your table.

And, finally, another option for formatting the borders in your table is to go to the Paragraph section of the Home tab, click on the Borders dropdown menu in the bottom right corner and either choose your line types if that's all you need or go to Borders and Shading to bring up the Borders and Shading dialogue box that will allow you to specify line color, weight, and type as well.

USING THE BORDER SAMPLER

If you have a line in a table that is formatted exactly the way you want already, you can sample it to copy its formatting. To do this, go to the Borders section of the Table Tools Design tab and click on the arrow under Border Styles. Then click on the Border Sampler option at the bottom of the dropdown. Your cursor will turn into a little eye dropper. Next, go to the line with the formatting you want and click on it. Word will take the formatting from that sample line and change the line style, weight, and color to match it. You can then apply that line style to the rest of your table or to other tables in your document.

(You can also access the Border Sampler by right-clicking on your table and choosing the Border Styles option and then choosing Border Sampler from there.)

CHANGE TEXT DIRECTION

By default, the text in the cells in a table will be aligned from left to right as if you were reading a line of text. If you would like it to instead be perpendicular to the normal direction of text, you can change this by going to the Table Tools Layout tab and clicking on Text Direction in the Alignment section on the right-hand side. There are only three options, and each click will change the direction of the text until you cycle back to normal.

ALIGN TEXT WITHIN A CELL

You can align text within a cell in a total of nine configurations. You can choose to place text either at the Top, Center, or Bottom of a cell and also to the Left, Center, or Right of the cell. To choose the combination you want, select the cells, go to the Alignment section of the Table Tools Layout tab and click on the image of the alignment you prefer. (If you only have one line of text in a cell, some of the alignment choices will appear to be identical.)

REPEAT A ROW AT THE TOP OF EACH PAGE

If you have a particularly long table that stretches across multiple pages, you should repeat the header row at the top of each page. Don't do this manually. One little edit and your whole document will be messed up. (Or one change to that header row and you'll have to make it on every single page. Ugh.)

To tell Word to repeat a row at the top of each page, click into one cell of the row, go to the Data section of the Table Tools Layout tab, and click on Repeat Header Rows. If you have more than one row you want to repeat, you can select cells in multiple rows and follow the steps above. The rows that repeat need to be the first ones in your table. You can't have the third row be the one that repeats. (Word won't let you click on the option unless it's the first row or row(s).)

Another way to specify that a row needs to repeat on each page is to click into a cell in the row you want to repeat, right-click, choose Table Properties, go to the Row tab, and click on Repeat As Header Row At The Top Of Each Page. You can do this for multiple rows at once, by selecting one cell from each row before you right-click.

TABLES:
OTHER

If you have tables that include a lot of data in them and you haven't completed your analysis, I'd recommend using Microsoft Excel for the analysis portion. For me, tables in Word are just to display information, they're not where you sort your information or analyze it. However, Word does allow for some manipulation of your data. So I'm going to cover it here, but it's not what I recommend doing. Excel is far better for this sort of thing than Word. And as long as you've built your table with the right number of rows and columns it's easy to copy and paste data from Excel into Word.

Anyway.

SORTING

You can actually sort lines of text in Word without having them in a table. You could have a list of five words in Word, each on a separate line, and have Word sort them by using the A to Z option in the Paragraph section of the Home tab. (Why you would ever do so, I don't know. But it is possible.)

It's far more likely, though, that you'd want to Sort entries in a table. For example, in the table above where I was listing information on books, maybe I'd realize after I'd created the table that I wanted to sort them by number of pages. Or by author name. Or by book title.

All are possible in Word.

To sort the entries in a table, select the whole table, go to the Table Tools Layout tab and click on the A to Z Sort option in the Data section on the right-hand side. It will bring up the Sort dialogue box.

If you have a header row in your table, tell Word and it will label your options using the labels in your header row. Otherwise it will just number the columns.

You can then choose to sort your table by the values in up to three different columns.

For each column you can choose to sort in either ascending or descending order and you can specify to Word whether the contents of the cells should be treated as text, numbers, or dates. The first column you list will be the main one used in the sort. The second listed column will only be used if two rows have the same value for the first column.

Your sort options here are not as sophisticated as those available in Excel, but for a basic sort, they're not bad.

FORMULAS

Again, I'd encourage you to use Excel for something like this. But if you don't want to listen to me, Word does have a formula option in the Table Tools Layout tab.

To use this option, click into a cell in your table and then go to the Table Tools Layout tab and click on Formula. This will bring up a Formula dialogue box. Word may suggest a formula to you based on the contents of the table, but it may not. If it doesn't, you can go down to the Paste function option at the bottom of the dialogue box and choose from the list of functions in the dropdown menu. That will paste an *empty* version of that function into the Formula line. You'll need to know what the function does (because there's nothing to explain it to you) and also be able to complete it yourself.

Here are a few options you can use:

=SUM(LEFT) will sum all numbers in columns to the left of the cell you're in

=AVERAGE(LEFT) will average the numeric values in the columns to the left of the cell you're in

=PRODUCT(LEFT) will multiply the numeric values in the columns to the left of the cell you're in

=COUNT(LEFT) will count the number of cells to the left of the one you're in that have numeric values

* * *

Note that for the formulas, Word only looks at numeric values. It won't count, for example, cells with text in them. You can change any of the above formulas to use RIGHT, ABOVE, and BELOW instead to apply the formulas to cells to the right in a row or above or below in a column.

To specify the format of your result, use the Number format dropdown choices in the dialogue box. Unfortunately, those number formats are only available for when you use a formula. So if you have a few columns with numbers you want to add in the final column, you can only format the final column where you add those values together. (Another reason to do most of this in Excel where you could format all of the columns the same.)

COMPARE TWO DOCUMENTS

That was tables. There's a lot to cover there and the next few topics are pretty complex, too, so I'm going to give things a bit of a break and talk about comparing documents for a minute which is something very useful, but not too hard to do.

Have you ever sent someone a document and had them return it to you with an "I only changed a few things" comment but had no idea what they changed? And been a little worried it was more than just a few things? (I have.)

Or have you ever had two versions of a document and not been sure what the difference between them was?

Well, document compare is a very easy way to compare two documents to see what was changed. (It uses track changes, but I consider it separate from track changes because I was using it long before track changes became what it is now.)

So. How do you compare two documents?

First, be sure that both documents you want to use have been saved. Word won't compare unsaved documents.

Next, open any document in Word. It can be one of the documents you want to use, but Word will make you find the documents you want to compare anyway, so it doesn't have to be. The key is to have Word open so you can access the Review tab.

Go to the Review tab and click on the dropdown under the Compare section and choose the Compare option. (We're not going to discuss Combine here. My super-attentive-to-detail self refuses to use it. There are just too many ways for a combine option to go wrong for me to trust it.)

When you choose the compare option, you will see the Compare Documents dialogue box.

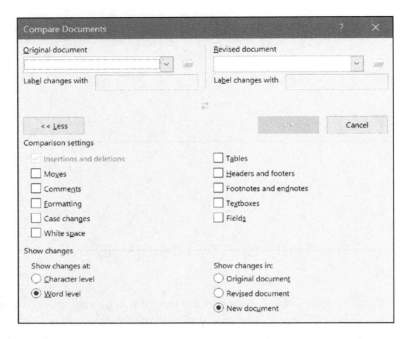

I've clicked on the More button here, but the default view just shows you the two dropdown menus where you choose which document to treat as the original and which to treat as the new document. Next to each of the dropdown menus is a small folder image. You can either see if the documents you need are in the dropdown or you can use the folder image to bring up a dialogue box that lets you navigate to where you have each document saved.

(Usually the dropdown is missing at least one of the documents I need, so I default to using the file image.)

Which document you list as the original and which you list as the revised document matters because Word will mark changes based upon what has been done to the document you identify as the original.

For example, take the following sentence:

"What are you doing here, Carl?"

Let's say the name was wrong and should've been Bob, so the person editing the document changed it. If you compare the documents in the correct order, Word will show something like this:

"What are you doing here, ~~Carl~~ Bob?"

See how (hopefully in ebook format, too) the Carl is struck out and replaced with Bob? If you compared the documents in the wrong order, Word would show Bob as the name that had been struck out.

So always be careful to select the correct original document and correct revised document.

As for the rest of the options there…

I never mess with the default settings on compare, they all work fine for me. But as you can see, there are a number of choices you can make about what to compare between the two documents.

After you select both of your documents, Word will show that it's going to label the changes between the documents as made by your Word user name. If you'd rather it showed those changes under a different name, change that before you hit OK.

Once you've made all of your choices, click on OK and Word will do the comparison. If you've left the other settings untouched, this will be done in a new document. Word will show the text of the original document in black text and any changes in the document with colored text. Deleted text will be shown as crossed out. From this point forward it will work just like track changes which we're going to talk about next.

Keep in mind that sometimes Word labels things as changes that really aren't. For example, I just ran Compare on a paperback I had recently reformatted and it's showing font changes that I hadn't technically made to the document. What I had done is accidentally deleted a header or two and had to retype the text. Even though I didn't change the font, Word labeled that as a font change.

Compare also doesn't do well if large chunks of text have been added or moved around. I've seen it miss that a paragraph of text was inserted into the document and then flag everything from that point forward as a change even though it really wasn't. (If that ever happens to you, I'd recommend creating a middle version of the document you're trying to compare to that has those large text blocks moved to where they are in the final and then running Compare. That way you still get to see the smaller changes that were made.)

Basically, it's a useful tool, but it's not perfect. So before you get ready to yell at someone for making changes to your document that they shouldn't have, go back to the original and the new version and confirm that the change you're upset about was actually made.

I should also add that I don't think I've ever had a situation where Compare failed to identify a change. When it errs it errs on the side of identifying more changes than there actually were.

Okay, time to talk about track changes so that you know how to look at the changes Compare flagged between your two documents.

TRACK CHANGES

I love track changes. It is a fantastic tool and I'm not sure how I lived without it before it existed. You can write a document, give it to a group for review, they can make their changes in track changes, and you can easily see what they did. It's wonderful.

But...

I've been putting off writing this part of the book because Track Changes is also somewhat finicky. And it's changed with different versions of Word. I know that copy and paste have pretty much stayed the same for the last twenty years, for example. But that's not true of track changes.

This is probably one of the tools in Word that they like to mess with the most between releases. So the version of track changes you have in your version of Word probably isn't the same as the version I have. Especially if you have Word 2016.

It's a vital tool so we have to cover it. Just go into this knowing that some of how this works (how changes are shown, for example) will be the same, but other parts of it (your default document view or how multiple reviewers are handled) won't be.

OVERVIEW

Let's start with the basics. What is track changes? It's a way for you to see what changes have been made in a document and by whom they were made and when they were made. (So no telling your boss you were working late editing that document when you weren't. One little look at track changes will show you were actually done by four.)

Track changes is a great way to make changes and see changes that were made to plain text in your document. It can be a disaster (at least in older versions) to use track changes when editing tables or numbered lists or when working on formatting.

In my opinion. (There will be some who strongly disagree with me, but I can't count the number of times I had to turn off track changes to wrestle a numbered list into shape or to really get a table looking the way it needed to. Not to mention, in some versions of Word changes to tables don't show as changes. You can delete a row or column and not have it shown as a change.)

So if you ever use track changes on a document, I highly recommend that you accept all changes in the document, turn off track changes entirely, and then do one final editing pass through the document. When I do this I inevitably find a few minor issues with formatting that need to be fixed and weren't readily visible in the track changes version. Like a double period at the end of a sentence or an extra space after a numbered list. (The newer your version of Word, the less likely you'll need to do this, but it's a good habit to develop. Also, it makes sure you've turned off track changes, which is something you really really want to do for all documents.)

HOW TO

To turn Track Changes on, open your document and go to the Review tab. Choose Track Changes from the Track Changes dropdown in the Tracking section.

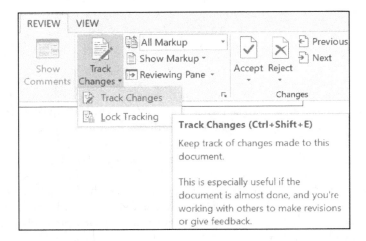

While track changes is turned on, any changes you make to the document will be tracked as a change to the document. Text that's been deleted will be shown as crossed out and be colored a different color based on the user who made the edit. Text that's been added will also be shown in a different color and underlined. For example:

> **This** is a test paragraph to sow you how track changes works. See how I misspelled show there?
>
> **This** is a test paragraph to show you how track changes works. See how I misspelled show there?
>
> When you make edits or add new text with track changes on, it looks something like this and a line appears on the left where changes were made.

Here I started with the first line of text and copied it. I then turned on track changes and added an h to the word show. It was marked in red and underlined. (Only for track changes. If I were to accept the change, that h I added would be in black text and without an underline, just like the text that surrounds it. This is one of the reasons I recommend accepting all changes and reading through your document one last time. I've seen text that was added to a document that was underlined by the user, but no one could tell that until all changes were accepted.)

You can also see in the example above where I deleted a question from what I had copied. That text is marked in red and crossed out.

The new text I added in the last paragraph is also marked in red.

Now, something to be aware of. I have worked with people who saw track changes, didn't understand how it works in Word, and so manually created their own version of track changes by formatting their edits to look like track changes. Rather than use track changes they would manually format the text they wanted to delete with a strikethrough, for example. That meant the text wasn't actually deleted. It was just reformatted.

NEVER, EVER DO THAT. Now that you've read this guide I expect you to understand that that is an awful way to show changes in your document. If you ever do that someone will have to manually go through the document and remove or reformat every single edit and they will hate you for it. Not to mention how much extra time and effort is required to do that. Just turn on track changes when you start to review the document and all of your edits will be recorded. If you mess it up and don't use track changes, then use Compare (discussed in the prior section) to have Word flag all of your edits for you. But never, never, never manually format your text to show the edits you want. That's something that was maybe necessary thirty years ago, but certainly is not now.

Also, if you're working with someone who isn't very familiar with Word, keep an eye out for this. I'm hoping we're past when people would do that, but we probably aren't. And the people most likely to do it are the most senior-level folks who you can't exactly make fix it themselves.

TRACK CHANGES VIEWS

It's the default in Word 2013 to show the final version of your document without the track changes visible and with only a small mark off to the side to indicate that a change has been made in the document. Personally, I hate that. I suppose it's good in theory because you get to see what the final product looks like without having to parse through what's been changed. And you're less likely to miss things like a double period that can be hard to catch when tracked changes are visible in the document.

But not being able to see the changes in a document can make reviewing edits tricky. At work I need to see each and every change made in a document to confirm that I agree, even the most minor one. In my day job area of expertise (financial regulation), it matters what words are used. Not to mention, comma placement can be crucial.

Because of this I always change my view so I can see the original version of the document with all changes visible.

(I also think it's important to remember that track changes are in place in a document. As you'll see in a second, there's a track changes view that doesn't show any indication that track changes are on. Problem with that view is if someone doesn't realize track changes are on and sends a document on to a client with those changes still in there and the client is able to see all of the changes. It can get ugly when that happens.)

Anyway.

There are four choices of view available in track changes. To access them, go to the Tracking section of the Review tab. You should see a dropdown menu on the top right of that section. Depending on your current view it will either say Simple Markup, No Markup, All Markup, or Original.

Here is an example of the text from above in each view.

Original

This is a test paragraph to sow you how track changes works. See how I misspelled show there?

This is a test paragraph to sow you how track changes works. See how I misspelled show there?

Simple Markup

This is a test paragraph to sow you how track changes works. See how I misspelled show there?

This is a test paragraph to show you how track changes works.

When you make edits or add new text with track changes on, it looks something like this and a line appears on the left where changes were made.

All Markup

This is a test paragraph to sow you how track changes works. See how I misspelled show there?

This is a test paragraph to s̲how you how track changes works. ~~See how I misspelled show there?~~

When you make edits or add new text with track changes on, it looks something like this and a line appears on the left where changes were made.

No Markup

This is a test paragraph to sow you how track changes works. See how I misspelled show there?

This is a test paragraph to show you how track changes works.

When you make edits or add new text with track changes on, it looks something like this and a line appears on the left where changes were made.

It may be a little hard to see, so let me also describe each view for you. Original shows what the text looked like before I turned on Track Changes. None of the changes that have been made in the document are visible. This can be a useful view if you want to see what a document looked like before people started mucking around with it, but that's really the only time you should use it.

Simple Markup has a red line off to the left side of the text. This line indicates that changes were made to the text on that line, but you can't tell what changes were made. The text you see on the page is the final text after all edits.

All Markup (my preferred view) has a line off to the left side of the text to indicate that changes have been made, but also shows those changes in the text of the document. So you can see that I've added text and deleted text and what text I've added and deleted.

No Markup is the most dangerous view in my opinion. It shows the final text with no indication that track changes is on or that changes have been made at that point in the document. It can have its uses. You can use it to see what the final document will look like with all changes incorporated. But I would highly, highly recommend that you never leave your document in this view. Use it and immediately change it back. And if you work with someone who uses this setting, be sure to always check any document before you send it on as a final document to make sure that track changes have been turned off and all changes in the document have been accepted.

SHOW MARKUP DROPDOWN

I should note that none of the views showed the formatting change I made to the word "This" in the first line. I bolded that text and yet none of them indicate that I did that. (In older versions of Word the change probably would be visible, but not in Word 2013.)

To see formatting changes in your document, go to the Tracking section of the Review pane and click on Show Markup to bring up the dropdown menu. From there go to Balloons which will bring up a secondary dropdown menu. Select the Show Only Comments And Formatting In Balloons option. This will add indications off to the side when formatting changes have been made in the document.

The default show markup view is Show All Revisions Inline which clearly doesn't work if you want to see formatting revisions. It also doesn't show comments (which we'll cover in a minute) in their entirety. They're just indicated by a small set of initials in brackets within the document. I would recommend always having your comments visible to the side since that's where a lot of the explanations and back and forth between reviewers occurs. (Or at least where it should.)

(Another show markup option is to Show Revisions in Balloons, which in my sample here looks exactly like Show Only Comments and Formatting In Balloons.)

If I change my view to show comments and formatting in balloons, it looks like this:

Now you can finally see all of the edits that have been made to the document with the indicator on the right-hand side showing that I bolded the word "This" in the document.

The way I would recommend you review any document is with All Markup selected and Comments and Formatting In Balloons selected. (And if you find you don't want to see formatting edits at all, you can turn that off in the Show Markup dropdown menu by clicking on formatting to uncheck it.) Only use the other options for very specific purposes and then always change it back.

CHANGES BY MULTIPLE USERS

Unless something is off about the settings on your document, each individual user who makes changes to the document will be assigned a different color for their changes. When it's just one person making edits to the document using track changes, those changes are generally shown in red. The next user is in blue, etc., etc. This isn't based on who the user is, so you can be assigned the color red in one document and green in another. If you hold your mouse over any specific change, Word will tell you who the user was who made the changes and when they made them.

(If your document has been stripped of personalization, it's possible to have all changes in the document show up under Author and to not be able to tell who made what change. I would highly recommend that you do not strip personalization from a document that you intend to continue working on. Or that if you have to do so that you also save a version that hasn't had personalization stripped. It's horrible to work on a group document when all changes are marked as by Author.)

Also, if for some reason someone hasn't customized their version of Word (which is rare in corporate settings and probably impossible in newer versions of Word) the changes they make will show up as Author. If you happen to have two users who have done this, their changes will be combined under the same color and user name.

REVIEWING PANES

Track changes also gives you the option of using something called reviewing panes. Review panes list all formatting changes, insertions, deletions, and comments. You can have one visible either below the document (horizontal) or off to the side of the document (vertical).

Usually reviewing panes aren't visible unless you choose to open them, but sometimes they will appear automatically. (I want to say this happens when there are so many comments in a section that they aren't easy to see otherwise.)

If you want to see a reviewing pane, go to the Tracking section of the Review tab and choose the type of reviewing pane you want from the Reviewing Pane dropdown menu. This will insert a new window on your screen that lists all of the changes that have been made to the document.

The reviewing panes can be useful, but I almost never use them. For example, when I bolded "This" the reviewing pane indicates that something was bolded at that point in the document, but it doesn't say what. Whereas when I turn on the option to see formatting change in a balloon there's a dotted line pointing to the text that was changed.

SEEING PREVIOUS AND NEXT CHANGES

Now that we have the settings the way we want them (for me that's all markup and comments and formatting in balloons), it's time to review the changes that were made in the document.

If I'm just reviewing changes to a document, I will walk through the document by using the Previous and Next options in the Changes section of the Review tab.

To do this, start at the beginning of your document and click Next. That will take you to the next change that was made in the document and will highlight it for you so you can review it. This approach lets you catch even the smallest edits. If you just scan your document for different colored text, you're very likely to miss changes to punctuation. (You can scan for the mark on the left-hand side of the page that indicates a change was made instead, but even that isn't perfect. If there was a larger edit and a smaller edit in the same paragraph you may only see the larger edit.)

And be sure to go through the entire document. If you don't start on the first page, you need to make sure you continue through to where you did start your review.

ACCEPT OR REJECT CHANGES

Using Previous and Next will show you the changes that were made in your document but will also leave them in the document still marked as changes.

The other option for walking through a document is to use the Accept or Reject options in the Changes section of the Review tab. This will accept or reject the changes as you review them and remove them from being visible changes to the document.

I generally don't use them this way. What I do is review all changes in a document and if I'm happy with all of them, and it's my role to do so, I accept all changes at the end of my review. If I run into a change I don't like, I'll make further edits to the document to make it acceptable or I'll reject it at that point.

But if you do want to accept changes as you move through the document, go to the Changes section of the Review tab, and click on the dropdown next to Accept. You'll see that you have a number of available options:

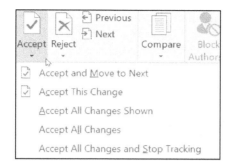

(The options for Reject are the same except using Reject in place of Accept.)

The option I would use if I was walking through a document and accepting changes as I went is Accept And Move To Next. This accepts the change you're currently on and moves to the next change in the document. If you reach a change that you don't want to keep, then you would choose Reject And Move To Next from the Reject dropdown.

If you're going to do it this way, be careful with sections that have multiple changes. Sometimes you'll accept a change but it won't accept all changes that were made to that section and you'll need to do it a few times to accept all of the changes. (Same goes for rejecting changes.)

Basically, if you're accepting or rejecting changes and you're not doing it for all changs at once, be sure that the text appears the way you want it to before you move on.

(I should note, too, that when using Previous and Next I have on occasion accepted all changes on a section to make sure that it will appear the way I expect and then used Ctrl + Z to undo that so I could just accept all changes once at the very end. You could probably use the No Markup view and get the same outcome.)

And one more note: Be careful when rejecting edits. If you review a document and reject an edit, Word doesn't show that an edit was made and then later rejected. So no one is going to know about that edit. It's just gone. When working on large group projects this can be a problem. I once saw someone very senior make an edit that was rejected by a junior staff member who thought they knew what they were doing and didn't. Because the edit and subsequent rejection of the edit didn't show in the document, no one on the team knew about it. Fortunately, someone else on the team caught the issue in a read-through, but that may not always happen. If I think it's important that someone see and approve it, I will edit an edit instead of reject it. (Or you can add a comment to the document indicating that you just rejected the edit.)

TURNING OFF TRACK CHANGES

Always turn off track changes when you're done with editing a document. There's nothing worse than making a few last-minute changes and having them show up in track changes and not catching it. (Okay, there are worse things. I've already mentioned a few in this guide. But still.)

To turn off track changes, go to the Tracking section of the Review tab and click on Track Changes to bring up the dropdown menu and then click on Track Changes. (You can also use Ctrl +

Shift + E to turn track changes on and off.)

If you still have changes tracked in your document, turning off track changes will leave those changes the way they are (marked as changes), but any edits you make to the document from that point forward will not show as changes. Be very careful about doing that, though. It's easy to turn off track changes and forget that you did it and then send on a document to someone else for review and have them not see all of the changes you made.

I do turn off track changes when I'm working on edits to complex multi-level lists and sometimes with tables, too, because it's just easier to work without track changes on, but when I do this I usually will run a document compare at the very end and provide that to anyone who needs to review my edits so that they can see all changes that were made.

TRACK CHANGES WITH TABLES, LISTS, AND FORMATTING

As I just mentioned, I tend to turn off track changes when I need to do a lot of formatting changes or when I'm working with tables or multi-level lists. One reason is because when you make a lot of formatting changes they can get overwhelming and generally don't matter to anyone else. No one needs to see that the spacing of that paragraph was changed, they just need to know it now matches the rest of the paragraphs. (And the folks that don't want to see all of that are usually also the ones that don't know how to turn it off themselves.)

The other main reason is because Word wasn't always as good at tracking changes as it is now. In older versions of Word I simply couldn't get tables or numbered lists to look like what I wanted if I was editing them in track changes. The minute I accepted all changes something would be off. (And I can't say with 100% certainty that there still aren't issues with newer versions of Word. So to save myself the headache, I turn it off, do what I need to do, and then do a document compare for anyone who needs to see what I've done.)

COMMENTS

I often think of comments in conjunction with track changes because that's where they tend to be used the most. For example, you make an edit in a document and want to say something about it to the others who are reviewing the document so put a comment off to the side. Or have a question about something someone said, so put the question in a comment.

But, actually, comments can be used separate from track changes. You can insert a comment into a document that has never had track changes turned on. And you definitely should use the comments function rather than add a comment or question into the text of a document where it doesn't belong.

Over the years I have seen people type a comment or question into the text of a document and then highlight it, put it in brackets [like this], underline it, or change the color of the text to set it apart from the rest of the text in the document. DO NOT DO THAT.

The only time I would say that is an acceptable thing to do is when you have information that is missing from your document and must be inserted into the document before you finalize it. So if you write, "The American Revolution occurred in [DATE] and was led by [NAME]", that's fine. Because you cannot and should not finalize the document until you fill in those bracketed portions.

But for comments like "do we really want to say this?", you don't want those left in the text accidentally. If you put them in a comment, there is an option to delete all comments from a document that will ensure they are removed before the document is finalized. (Assuming someone uses it, of course.)

To insert a comment, click on the location in the document where you want your question or comment to appear and then go to the Review tab and under the Comments section click on New Comment. If you have your view set up the way I do, a comment box will appear on the right-hand side with your name and the time as well as a cursor on the next line. Type your comment or question and then click back into your document.

(Comments can't be used in footnotes. The only option you have is to add them near the footnote in your text or towards the bottom of the page where the footnote is located.)

If you don't have your view set up the way I do, a Reviewing Pane will open instead. It will show your name and Commented on one line with a cursor on the next line for you to type your comment or question. The existence of your comment will be indicated in the document itself by your initials in brackets. To see the text of a comment that isn't visible off to the side of the document, hold your cursor over the initials and it will appear in a comment bubble.

To reply to a comment someone has made, you can click into that comment box and add your thoughts. (Not recommended.) Or you can click on a location next to where that comment was made and make a comment of your own. If who said what is important, make a new comment because Word doesn't distinguish within a comment box between who made the original comment and any edits that were later made to that comment.

To move between comments you can use the Previous and Next options in the Comments section of the Review tab.

If you want to review comments as part of reviewing changes in the document, use the Previous and Next options in the Changes section of the Review tab instead. That will take you through all changes, including any comments.

Also, since comments are treated separately from track changes, accepting all changes or rejecting all changes and turning off track changes will not remove the comments from the document. To remove comments you need to go to the Comments section of the Review tab and under the Delete option choose Delete All Comments In Document.

If you used comments in your document at any point it is always a best practice to check that comments have been deleted before finalizing the document.

MULTILEVEL LISTS

I saved multilevel lists for last because I truly hate working with them. At their most basic they are wonderful and a God-send. But when you're working for a company that requires its own custom version of a multilevel list with non-standard levels and bizarre indents, they're a nightmare to set up and a nightmare to get others to use properly. Which means hours wasted trying to fix them.

In *Word for Beginners* we covered basic numbered lists and bullet-pointed lists. Both are available from the Paragraph section of the Home tab on the top row, left side. What I skipped at that time was the third option in that row, multilevel lists.

Multilevel lists are essentially a more complex version of numbered lists that use various letters and numbering to provide a standard outline format. Like this:

I.	**Level One Item**
A.	*Level Two Item*
1.	Level Three Item
a)	**Level Four Item**

Word provides a number of pre-formatted choices you can use to create one of these lists.

The problem is, they never seem to be what you want them to be. Like the one I used above. The first three levels are fine, but then it goes for the lower-case a with a paren instead of a lower-case a with a period which is what I'd expect.

That might seem like a silly distinction to make. I mean, really, who cares if you use a paren instead of a period? Well, let me tell you...Lots of managers do. I've worked for companies that have spent *hundreds of thousands* of dollars on petty little differences like this. (And I will also admit that my mild obsessive compulsive tendencies are also annoyed by it.)

So there's that. The templates that Word oh so helpfully provides aren't ones you can use in most situations.

The other issue I have with them is that they change formatting in other parts of your document when you're not looking. When I started to write this section, I made the mistake of creating that example of a multilevel list that I used above in this document. Word changed all of my chapter headers. It converted all of them over to the formatting for level one items on that list because they use the Heading 1 style. Suddenly every single chapter heading in this document was numbered. All because I tried to use a pre-built multilevel list in one section of my document.

Now, I'm not saying don't use multi-level lists. I'm just saying be very careful if you do choose to use them. Ideally, do not use any other numbering or bulleting or headers in a document that uses them. They have to provide the entire structure of your document or you'll end up spending hours fixing your document.

So.

If you do need to use a multilevel list, how do you do it?

Let me tell you a way to avoid using them altogether first. Then we'll dive into using the actual multilevel list option.

If you insert a numbered list into Word (using the Numbering option in the Paragraph tab that was discussed in *Word for Beginners*), you can turn that list into a list with multiple levels by using the tab key or the increase indent option.

To do this, start your first line with a capital I followed by a period and a space. Word will automatically convert that to the first entry in a numbered list. Type a value for that first entry. It doesn't have to be your final text, but you do need text on this line. (Otherwise if you hit enter it will disappear.)

Now, hit enter. Word will automatically continue the numbered list and start the next row with the number two (II) followed by a period and space. To create a secondary level for your multilevel list, hit Tab or use the Increase Indent option in the Paragraph section of the Home tab.

Word will turn that two (II) into a lower-case a. When you type text into that line and hit enter, it will number the next row with a lower-case b. (You can use Shift + Tab or Decrease Indent from the Paragraph section of the Home tab to move back one level to a II.)

Or you can create a third level for your list that will be numbered with lower-case roman numerals (i, ii, iii, etc.) by using tab or increasing the indent.

If at any point using the tab keys or the indent options doesn't change the list level, type some text on that line and then go to the beginning of the text and try again. Sometimes, for whatever reason, Word will only change the list level if there's already text entered on that line and then only if you position your cursor at the start of where the text is.

If you do what I just described, you can get a multilevel list that looks like this and is pretty easy to work with:

I. Heading One

   a. Heading Two

     i. Heading Three

       1. Heading Four

Problem is, that's not standard format. Usually you'd expect to see the upper-case Roman numeral (I) followed by an upper case letter A and then lower-case versions of both. That lower-case a in the second level is incorrect.

You can try to force the list into standard format by going to each level of the list and choosing the appropriate letter/number and format for that level, but then the spacing between the number and the text becomes inconsistent and using the indent options stops working. You can fix these things, but they're not stable and will sometimes revert to their old formatting unexpectedly. You'll change an indent on page ten and the indent on page two will go back to its original form with no warning or notice. The only way you'll know is by looking back through your document.

The other option you have, of course, is the multilevel list option.

To create a multilevel list, type in the text you want for your first entry, click on that line of text, and choose an option from the multilevel list options.

Unlike with the Numbering option, you can't just hit enter and have the next line automatically be included in the list. When you hit enter, you'll be back to plain text. To change that next line to part of the list, once again select the list from the multilevel list dropdown. If you want this line to be indented one level, you can use the tab key or the indent option once you've chosen the list from the menu.

The nice thing about each line not being automatically included in the list is that this lets you have sections of text underneath each entry in your list. Like this:

> ## I. Heading One
> So this is where you'd discuss the key parts covered by this section in your document.
>
> ### a. Heading Two
> And then you'd add more text that talks about the first subpoint in that discussion.
>
> #### i. Heading Three
> And more text that discusses the subpoint of that subpoint.

You can do this with the other approach as well, but the multilevel list option seems especially designed for this. And if you're using one of Word's pre-defined lists, it works fairly well. Spacing and formatting is consistent across the various levels.

What I do when I'm using one of these lists is I set up the number of levels I need (for example, above I have three levels) and then I use the Format Painter to assign the correct level to the other headers in my document. You can also use the multilevel list dropdown, just be sure you click on the list under Lists In Current Documents to be sure that you're actually using the same list throughout the whole document.

The tricky part to using these lists comes when you decide you want to use your own multilevel list with either custom numbering or custom formatting. I had a client who had a very, very specific list they wanted to use but had no documents set up with it, so users were constantly trying to recreate it in each new report they wrote and it took hours to get it right. The only way I ever found to make those reports work consistently was to start with a brand-new document where I'd created the multilevel list to their specifications and then copying in the text for each section, being careful to strip out any numbering or list in each copied section. Trying to build a custom multilevel list in a document that has already used a numbered list just doesn't work well.

If you ever do need to build a custom multilevel list, the option is there under the multilevel list dropdown. Click on Define New Multilevel List and it will bring up the Define New Multilevel List dialogue box.

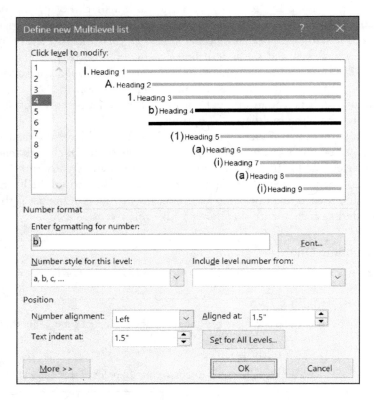

Defining each level of your list is pretty straightforward. Click on each level, choose the numbering style you want to use for that level, and then set your indents. Word will show you a preview of how all the levels you've set look. The problem is getting the lists to be stable within a Word document and to not have them revert to an unwanted format. All I can say is be sure to use any custom list you build in a new document and to only use that list. Don't try to combine different numbered lists in the same document when you're working with a custom multi-level list.

FOOTNOTES AND ENDNOTES

One more that I think you'll run into often enough that we should cover it is footnotes and endnotes. Footnotes go at the bottom of the page. Endnotes go at the end of the document or the section. Other than that, they're pretty similar in how they work and how you insert them into your document.

To insert a footnote or endnote, position your cursor at the location in the document where you want to place it and go to the Footnotes section of the References tab. Click on either Insert Footnote or Insert Endnote. Here's an example of a footnote that I inserted into a document:

> As you may have noticed, I like to make side comments a lot. I usually do them in parens within the text of the document, but another way to handle that would be to insert a footnote or endnote.[i]
>
> ---
>
> [i] _Like this one._

See how it's separated from the main text of the document by a short line and then numbered with a superscript number 1 and how there is also a superscript number one in the main body text to indicate what the footnote is referring to?

The default is for the text of the footnote to be in the the same font as the main body text but in a slightly smaller (10 point versus 11 point) font size. If you want to change that, you can change the style of the footnote or you can simply edit the footnote like you would normal text. (Unlike headers and footers, you don't have to double-click to access a footnote or endnote.) If you edit it like normal text, select the text and then use the options in the Font section of the Home tab or right-click and open the Font dialogue box.

If you want to change the style of your footnote, you can right-click on the footnote and choose Style from the dropdown menu. This will bring up a Style box that includes a basic summary of the font and font size, etc. that are used for footnotes. Click on Modify and that will bring you to the standard Modify Style dialogue box where you can change the style for all of your footnotes at once.

What you see above is the standard appearance and format for a footnote. If you want more control over your footnotes and/or endnotes, you can click on the expansion arrow in the bottom right corner of the Footnotes section of the References tab to bring up the Footnote and Endnote dialogue box. This allows you to change where the footnotes and endnotes display as well as how they're numbered. This is also where you can choose to convert your footnotes to endnotes or vice versa.

(To convert an individual footnote or endnote to the other option, you can right-click on that specific footnote or endnote and choose the Convert To [X] option from the dropdown menu.)

If you need to delete a footnote or endnote, you have to do so in the document itself. Deleting the text of the footnote or endnote will still leave the number in your document. Selecting and deleting the small superscripted number in your text will delete both the number and the contents of the footnote/endnote.

Be careful if you have footnotes or endnotes in your document and you're copying and pasting sections or changing the font or font size that you don't also change the font and font size for the numbering of the footnotes and endnotes. I know this can happen in older versions of Word, although I wasn't able to replicate it in Word 2013 when I tried to do so.

If you have track changes turned on and you edit the text in an endnote or footnote, those edits will show in track changes. However, you cannot tie a comment to an endnote or a footnote. The best you can do is put the comment close to the location of the endnote or footnote.

Also, when you're reading a document, if you want to see what the text of a footnote or endnote is without going to the end of the page or end of the section or document, you can do so by holding your cursor over the number of the footnote or endnote.

HOW TO FIND OTHER ANSWERS

So that's it. That's all we're going to cover in this guide.

There are, however, a number of other things that Word can do. Things like mail merges and page borders and changing your page color or adding text effects.

My goal with this guide was to keep it to a manageable level and focus on what most people will need most of the time. But now that you've walked through it you should hopefully be starting to see that Word has a certain logic to it. Even if we didn't cover a specific topic you should feel comfortable enough by now to try to use it and see what it does and how it works.

But if you need a little more guidance than that, I want to walk you through how to find it.

First, if you see an option in the Word toolbar that you want to know more about, you can try holding your cursor over it. Often this will give you a brief description of what the option does. Like this one for SmartArt from the Insert tab that says it's a way to insert a graphic to visually communicate information.

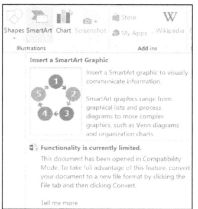

Sometimes those descriptions will also have a Tell Me More option at the bottom. (For example, the Hyperlink description has one that relates to inserting a hyperlink.)

Clicking on Tell Me More will bring up the help screen for that particular function or topic. This may be all you need. Or not.

You can also access the help screen directly by clicking on the small question mark in the top right corner or pressing the F1 key. Once there, you can enter the search term you're interested in, hit enter, and then click on one of the search results to read more about it.

Usually the in-product help screens don't provide me with the answers I need, so I turn to the internet. I always start with the Microsoft website because it usually does have what I need.

I do an Internet search for something like "SmartArt Word 2013" that references my version of the product and the topic I'm interested in, and then I click on the support.office.com search result. If you're trying to figure out how something works in Word, this will usually bring you to a nice page with a step-by-step description that includes screenshots.

If that doesn't work, because maybe you need to know how to do something specific, there are a number of internet user forums where people discuss how to perform various tasks in Word and also a number of blogs where people have posted about how to perform various tasks. A quick internet search on what you're trying to do, "mail merge Word 2013" for example, should bring up a number of possible results.

You can also post a question in a user forum, but beware that you may receive a few snide comments back if you don't provide a very clear question that explains exactly what you need to do and what version of the program you're using.

If you do find an answer on a forum or a blog, be careful. Don't click on random links posted by random strangers on the internet. That's a good way to get a virus. And don't give someone you don't trust remote access to your computer either. Or open a file they send you. Basically, don't be too trusting. If someone can't describe to you how to do something then maybe they don't know what they're talking about.

Also, you can always ask me. I'll either tell you, if I know the answer, or try to find it for you. My email is mlhumphreywriter@gmail.com. I can't guarantee I'll be able to answer every single question, but I can probably handle most of them. And be forewarned that I don't check that account daily, but I do check it regularly so you may not get an immediate response, but you will get one. (Just don't ask for my help with a broken multilevel list. That you'd have to pay me good money to fix because I seriously hate working with them. Also, I try not to open documents from strangers…)

So there you have it. By now you should know 99% of what you need to know and be comfortable enough to find the answers to that other 1%.

I hope this book was helpful and best of luck.

INDEX

CONTROL SHORTCUTS

For each of the control shortcuts, hold down Ctrl and the key listed to perform the command.

Command	Ctrl +
Select All	A
Bold	B
Copy	C
Center	E
Find	F
Replace	H
Italicize	I
Print	P
Save	S
Underline	U
Paste	V
Cut	X
Redo	Y
Undo	Z

ABOUT THE AUTHOR

M.L. Humphrey is a former stockbroker with a degree in Economics from Stanford and an MBA from Wharton who has spent close to twenty years as a regulator and consultant in the financial services industry.

You can reach M.L. at mlhumphreywriter@gmail.com or at mlhumphrey.com.

www.ingramcontent.com/pod-product-compliance
Lightning Source LLC
LaVergne TN
LVHW062318060326
832902LV00013B/2291